Whatever is Lovely

Adessa Holden

WHATEVER IS LOVELY

Copyright © 2025 4ONE MINISTRIES, INC

All rights reserved. No portion of this book may be reproduced, stored in a retrieval system, or transmitted in any form or by any means—electronic, mechanical, photocopy, recording, scanning, or other—except for brief quotations in reviews or articles, without the prior written permission of the author.

Published by 4One Ministries, Inc. Visit www.adessaholden.com for more information on bulk discounts and special promotions, or e-mail your questions to info@4oneministries.org.

The ESV® Bible (The Holy Bible, English Standard Version®). ESV® Text Edition: 2016. Copyright © 2001 by Crossway, a publishing ministry of Good News Publishers. The ESV® text has been reproduced in cooperation with and by permission of Good News Publishers. Unauthorized reproduction of this publication is prohibited. All rights reserved.

The Holy Bible, New International Version®, NIV®. Copyright ©1973, 1978, 1984, 2011 by Biblica, Inc.™ Used by permission of Zondervan. All rights reserved worldwide. www.zondervan.com The "NIV" and "New International Version" are trademarks registered in the United States Patent and Trademark Office by Biblica, Inc.™

Scripture quotations marked KJV are taken from the King James Version®. King James Version. Dallas, TX: Brown Books Publishing, 2004. Used by permission. All rights reserved.

Scripture quotations marked (NLT) are taken from the Holy Bible, New Living Translation, copyright © 1996, 2004, 2007 by Tyndale House Foundation. Used by permission of Tyndale House Publishers, Inc., Carol Stream, Illinois 60188. All Scripture taken from the New Century Version®. Copyright © 2005 by Thomas Nelson. Used by permission. All rights reserved.

Scripture quotations from THE MESSAGE. Copyright © by Eugene H. Peterson 1993, 1994, 1995, 1996, 2000, 2001, 2002. Used by permission of NavPress. All rights reserved. Represented by Tyndale House Publishers, Inc.

Scripture taken from the New King James Version®. Copyright © 1982 by Thomas Nelson. Used by permission. All rights reserved.

Design: James J. Holden

Subject Headings:
1. Christian life 2. Women's Ministry 3. Spiritual Growth

ISBN 978-1-965809-04-4

Printed in the United States of America

WHAT PEOPLE ARE SAYING ABOUT *WHATEVER IS LOVELY:*

"***Whatever is Lovely*** is a timely and much-needed resource that speaks with both grace and truth. The use of Scripture throughout is strong and consistent, always pointing the reader back to the Word of God—a crucial anchor when dealing with such a sensitive topic.

The inclusion of both group study questions and private reflection prompts shows real discernment, offering space for women to process in the way that best suits their journey.

What I appreciated most is that the book doesn't stop at the *"why,"* but also equips readers with practical tools for the *"how."* From implementing parental controls to removing internet access altogether, the suggestions are clear, doable, and deeply helpful for those seeking real change!

Whatever is Lovely is a valuable resource for women ready to walk in freedom." —**Pastor Nichole Schreiber,** *Lead Pastor, Erie First Assembly of God & At-Large Female Presbyter, PennDel Ministry Network*

"***Whatever is Lovely*** is a practical, personal, and powerful tool for a woman who battles with private sexual sins." —**Charisse Jenkins,** *Women's Director, PennDel Ministry Network*

"***Whatever is Lovely*** is an excellent resource for any pastor! Adessa does a wonderful job of verbalizing Scriptural truths to women concerning purity, freedom from sexual addictions, ways to pursue holiness, and setting minds on things that are honorable.

It is written without causing shame or condemnation, but rather with words of encouragement - that it IS possible to transform your mind & grow in your walk with Christ!"
—**Pastor Jen Ferguson**, *Lead Pastor, New Covenant Assembly of God*

"Now more than ever, the church needs resources that tackle tough issues from a biblical perspective.

Adessa Holden has created a powerful and practical tool for individuals and church leaders leading discipleship groups.

I am thankful that 4One Ministries chooses to confront truth boldly while addressing challenging topics with love and grace." —**Lori Cullen**, *Worship Pastor, Philadelphia Christian Center, 4One Ministries Board Member*

DEDICATION

This book is dedicated to Devi Titus, an author, speaker, Bible teacher, women's minister, and the pastor's wife at my church when I was a teen.

Thank you for setting an example for me of what it means to be a strong, godly woman in ministry who doesn't shy away from difficult topics but teaches uncompromising Biblical truth. I'll always remember what you taught about keeping our hearts and minds pure and focusing on the things that are true, pure, and lovely. I will never forget you and always be glad you were in my life.

Table of Contents

1	You Are Not Alone	9
2	Is God Against Sex?	27
3	Coming Out Of The Dark	47
4	Creating A Battle Plan	63
5	Tools To Help You Overcome	83
6	You Gotta Fight For Your Right To Purity	103
7	Final Thoughts	123
	Bibliography	129
	Resources	131

Chapter One
You Are Not Alone

So here's an odd fact about my life: In the fifteen years that my brother and I have been serving in ministry, I have attended more Men's Conferences than Women's Conferences. (And I've been to a lot of women's conferences.) In my position working for my brother, managing the registration and book sales at Mantour Ministries, I've noticed a few differences between the two events.

First, men do not dress up for conferences, while women usually wear their hippest, trendiest outfits. (At least on the first day. By the last day, things are more relaxed, but on day one, most women look good.)

Men love donuts and bacon and will eat as much of either as the conference offers. The big features at women's events are chocolate and really good coffee.

Here's a big difference: At almost every men's event I've ever attended, there is an entire session dedicated to the topic of overcoming pornography and sexual temptation. Yet, it's a topic that's rarely, if ever, addressed at women's events.

I've often asked myself, *"Why?"*

While I don't have all the answers to this question, I believe one reason is that too many Christians have fallen for the lie that pornography and sexual sin are mainly masculine issues.

It's a guy problem—not something many women struggle to overcome.

Yet, nothing is further from the truth.

- 33 % of young adult women use pornography monthly.[1]
- More than half of women 25 and under ever seek out porn (56% versus 27% among women 25-plus), and one-third seek it out at least monthly.[2]
- 17% of women consider themselves addicted to pornography.[1]
- *XXXchurch*, an online Christian resource for porn addicts, cites that 1 in 3 visitors to adult sites are women, 9.4 million women view porn monthly, and 13 percent of women admit accessing porn at work. [3]
- 70% of all women keep their cyber activities a secret.[4]
- 1 in 3 visits to all adult websites are women.[4]
- A recent study pointed out that while men use porn more than women — both genders still struggle with it. Around 75% of Christian men and 40% of Christian women reported consuming porn on some level.[5]

These numbers don't include the women who are so covered in shame from this struggle that they don't answer truthfully. They also don't include the even more significant number of women who don't consider the *"soft porn"* they watch on television, movies, view on

You Are Not Alone

social media, or read in romance novels to be a problem.

And it isn't just a problem with non-Christian women. The numbers inside the church are still pretty high. 87% of Christian women have watched pornography.[1]

The truth is that pornography, sexual sin, and sexual addiction are not just men's issues. Many women inside and outside of the church are entangled in this trap. Some are trying to overcome it but don't know how. They've tried repeatedly to break free, only to fall into temptation again. Many feel that they are alone in their struggle and are too ashamed to reach out and ask for help. After all, women aren't supposed to struggle with this issue.

While myriads of teaching and resources are available to help men, where is a woman to go?

When a man admits this struggle, there is a level of shame, but there's also an acceptance that this is a battle every man fights. There's even an excellent book titled *"Every Man's Battle"*. With that acceptance comes compassion. However, it's different for women. The lie that *"pornography is a man's problem"* has actually created a stigma that keeps women trapped.

Pornography, sexual sin, and sexual addiction are not just men's issues. Many women inside and outside of the church are entangled in this trap.

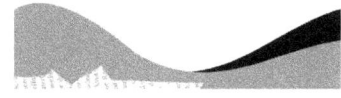

If you are a woman struggling with these issues, the first thing you need to know is that you are not alone. Now more than ever before, pornography, sexual temptation, sexual sin, and even sexual addiction are issues for both genders.

The statistics we started with prove it's true. Throughout our world, inside and outside of the church, women are struggling with these issues and looking for answers. That is why I believe the Holy Spirit led me to write this Bible study—to help women find freedom and to provide them with hope.

- Hope that you can be free.

- Hope that you can overcome.

- Hope that just because it seems like this sin controls your heart and mind and it's impossible to break free, that nothing is impossible with God. (Matthew 19:26)

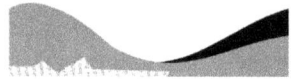

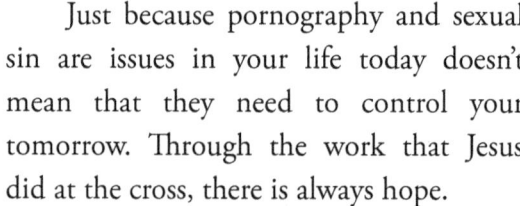

Just because pornography and sexual sin are issues in your life today doesn't mean that they need to control your tomorrow.

Just because pornography and sexual sin are issues in your life today doesn't mean that they need to control your tomorrow. Through the work that Jesus did at the cross, there is always hope.

This hope is displayed in John 4 and the story of the woman at the well. Let's take a moment to set the stage.

> *Jesus knew the Pharisees had heard that he was baptizing and making more disciples than John (though Jesus himself didn't baptize them—his disciples did). So he left Judea and returned to Galilee.*
>
> *He had to go through Samaria on the way. Eventually he came to the Samaritan village of Sychar, near the field that Jacob gave to his son Joseph.*
>
> *Jacob's well was there; and Jesus, tired from the long walk, sat wearily beside the well about noontime.*
>
> *Soon a Samaritan woman came to draw water, and Jesus said to her, "Please give me a drink."*
>
> *He was alone at the time because his disciples had gone into the village to buy some food. -John 4:1-8 (NLT)*

The disciples have gone to get some food, leaving Jesus alone at a well in Sychar. As He was there, a woman came to the well, also alone. It's important to understand that this was unusual—it was customary for the women in the town to go to the well together during the cooler parts of the day. So why was this woman coming alone at noon?

The answer came out during her conversation with Jesus. She was carrying the shame of her sexual sin.

> *"Go and get your husband," Jesus told her.*
>
> *"I don't have a husband," the woman replied.*
>
> *Jesus said, "You're right! You don't have a husband-for you have had five husbands, and you aren't even married to the man you're living with now. You certainly spoke the truth!" -John 4:16-18 (NLT)*

Like so many who went before and even more who came after her, the Samaritan woman was trapped in a cycle of sexual sin. We don't know the details—we don't need to know the details—we know the essential facts.

First, she was hiding and covered in shame because of her sexual sin.

More importantly, her encounter with Jesus changed her life and set her free. How do we know this? Let's jump ahead and read the next few verses.

> *"Sir," the woman said, "you must be a prophet. So tell me, why is it that you Jews insist that Jerusalem is the only place of worship, while we Samaritans claim it is here at Mount Gerizim, where our ancestors worshiped?"*
>
> *Jesus replied, "Believe me, dear woman, the time is*

> *coming when it will no longer matter whether you worship the Father on this mountain or in Jerusalem. You Samaritans know very little about the one you worship, while we Jews know all about him, for salvation comes through the Jews. But the time is coming—indeed it's here now—when true worshipers will worship the Father in spirit and in truth. The Father is looking for those who will worship him that way.*
>
> *For God is Spirit, so those who worship him must worship in spirit and in truth."*
>
> *The woman said, "I know the Messiah is coming—the one who is called Christ. When he comes, he will explain everything to us."*
>
> *Then Jesus told her, "I am the Messiah!"*
>
> *Just then his disciples came back. They were shocked to find him talking to a woman, but none of them had the nerve to ask, "What do you want with her?" or "Why are you talking to her?"*
>
> *The woman left her water jar beside the well and ran back to the village, telling everyone, "Come and see a man who told me everything I ever did! Could he possibly be the Messiah?"*
>
> *So the people came streaming from the village to see him. -John 4:19-30 (NLT)*

I love this passage! It's so relatable! One of my favorite parts is the woman at the well's reply as Jesus gets to the heart of the issue of shame in her life. She does what so many of us do and tries to sound super religious. But Jesus doesn't want to talk about religion.

Instead, He moves the conversation toward telling her Who He is

—the Messiah— and what He can do to change her life.

We also see that, more than anything, the Samaritan woman wants what Jesus has to offer.

That's when we see the most amazing thing happen. The conversation ends when the disciples return with the food. However, the story doesn't end there—it's taking a dramatic turn. Because somewhere during her encounter with Jesus, she experienced a revolution. Something inside of her changed.

Now, instead of hiding in shame, she's actually going back into the town seeking people out. Rather than avoiding people because of her shame, she's telling everyone who will listen, *"I just met a Man Who told me everything I've ever done—He's the Messiah!"*

Because of her encounter with Jesus, her life was completely changed. What was formerly her shame was now her testimony as she fulfilled God's plan for her life-becoming the catalyst for revival in her town.

Here's the thing—while times have changed and the methods and opportunities for sexual temptation and sin have changed—the power of God to change lives has not changed.

The same Jesus that changed the life of the woman at the well wants to lift every woman who is caught in sexual sin out of their shame and give them a new life. Through the work that Jesus did at the cross, anyone can break the cycle, overcome whatever has you bound, and win the battle over sexual sin.

The same Jesus that changed the life of the woman at the well wants to lift every woman who is caught in sexual sin out of their shame and give them a new life.

Here's another powerful truth: **God wants you to be free.**

It breaks His heart to see you bond in sin that is damaging your relationship with Him and damaging your soul. Like the Father in the story of the prodigal son (Luke 15:11-32), He wants nothing more than for you to come to Him, repent of your sin, and ask Him to help you find freedom.

> *For the Lord your God is gracious and compassionate. He will not turn his face from you if you return to him. -2 Chronicles 30:9, (NIV)*

> *Repent, then, and turn to God, so that your sins may be wiped out, that times of refreshing may come from the Lord.-Acts 3:19 (NIV)*

Not only that, but Jesus is literally in Heaven right now, interceding for you and praying that you will overcome temptation.

> *Therefore he is able, once and forever, to save those who come to God through him. He lives forever to intercede with God on their behalf. -Hebrews 7:25 (NLT)*

> *So then, since we have a great High Priest who has entered heaven, Jesus the Son of God, let us hold firmly to what we believe. This High Priest of ours understands our weaknesses, for he faced all of the same testings we do, yet he did not sin.*

> *So let us come boldly to the throne of our gracious God. There we will receive his mercy, and we will find grace to help us when we need it most. -Hebrews 4:14-16 (NLT)*

As a child of God, you also have the Holy Spirit living inside of you, convicting you of sin and empowering you to overcome temptation.

> *The Spirit of God, who raised Jesus from the dead, lives in you. -Romans 8:11 (NLT)*

But let's go back a couple of verses in Romans 8 and see how this applies to overcoming sin:

> *But you are not controlled by your sinful nature.*
>
> *You are controlled by the Spirit if you have the Spirit of God living in you. (And remember that those who do not have the Spirit of Christ living in them do not belong to him at all.)*
>
> *And Christ lives within you, so even though your body will die because of sin, the Spirit gives you life because you have been made right with God.*
>
> *The Spirit of God, who raised Jesus from the dead, lives in you. And just as God raised Christ Jesus from the dead, he will give life to your mortal bodies by this same Spirit living within you.*
>
> *Therefore, dear brothers and sisters, you have no obligation to do what your sinful nature urges you to do.*
> *-Romans 8:9-12 (NLT)*

Did you see it?

Because the Holy Spirit lives inside of you, you can fight and overcome the power of sin in your life. Because you have experienced the transforming power of salvation, you don't need to stay broken by the same old sins in your life. Instead, with the help of the Holy Spirit living inside you, you have all you need to fight and overcome any sin in your life.

When temptation comes, you can resist.

When you want to fall back into a familiar sin, you don't have to.

Instead, filled with the power of the Holy Spirit and armed with the sword of the Spirit, which is the Word of God, you fight and win even a fight as difficult as the battle to overcome sexual sin.

Hebrews also tells us that there is a great cloud of witnesses in Heaven cheering for you, saying, *"Just like we overcame temptation, you can do it, too. We're pulling for you and believe you can do it."* (Hebrews 12:1)

Many women who have gone before you—women who know what it is like to be caught in the trap of pornography, lust, sexual temptation, and sexual sin—have overcome and lived the rest of their lives in freedom. They are a cloud of witnesses, wanting you to know that there is hope.

Today, they stand as testimonies that the same power of God that worked in the life of the Samaritan woman still works today.

This same hope is available to any woman who is struggling with any form of sexual addiction. Whether you are addicted to soft porn on television or in romance novels, hardcore porn on the internet, pornographic videos on social media, or any other form of pornography. Even if you're living a sexually sinful lifestyle, there is hope for you.

The truths of this chapter are simple: you are not alone.

The traps of pornography, lust, and sexual sin are not male problems. Since the beginning of time, women have struggled with sexual sin.

The good news is that, like the woman at the well, many women have also overcome, gained freedom, and chosen to walk in purity through the power of God. Each one of them stands as a testimony, saying, *"You can do it. There is hope."*

The only question that remains is: *"Do you want to overcome? Do you want to experience freedom?"*

Do you want to have the testimony of the woman at the well who said, *"This is how I used to be and what I used to do, but through the power of Jesus, I have a new life?"*

If you answered, *"yes,"* then I encourage you to get alone with Jesus and tell Him that you want to be free. Pour out your heart and tell Him about your struggle, but also about your desire for a new life.

Ask Him to forgive you and help you as you move forward.

Then, move on to the next chapter, where we'll start talking about the road to complete freedom.

 ## Group Study Questions...

1. How do you define *"pornography"*?

2. Were you surprised by the statistics in this chapter? Did you think it would be more or less women using pornography?

3. How does the belief that *"pornography is a man's problem"* create a stigma that keeps women from getting help?

4. Go back and read John 4:1-30. How did Jesus interact with the Samaritan woman? How did He talk to her? What were His attitudes?

5. Read Luke 15:11-32. How did the father respond when the prodigal son returned and repented? What does this teach us about God's heart when we repent from our sins—including sexual sin?

Questions to Answer Privately....

1. Do you struggle with pornography, including the *"soft porn"* women watch on television, movies, social media, and novels?

2. How often do you use pornography? Would you consider yourself addicted to pornography?

3. Are you actively participating in any other type of sexual sin?

4. How did you feel reading the statistics about women and pornography?

5. Do you ever feel shame or guilt from the stigma that pornography, lust, and sexual sin are primarily male issues?

6. What did you personally take from the story of the Samaritan woman?

7. Is it easier for you to see God as angry at you for your sin?

8. How do you feel about this sentence: *"Because the Holy Spirit lives inside of you, you can fight and overcome the power of sin in your life. Because you have experienced the transforming power of salvation, you don't need to stay broken by the same old sins in your life. Instead, with the help of the Holy Spirit living inside you, you have all you need to fight and overcome any sin in your life."*?

9. Do you want to overcome? Do you want to experience freedom? Do you want to have the testimony of the woman at the well who said, *"This is how I used to be and what I used to do, but through the power of Jesus, I have a new life?"* Are you ready to do whatever it takes to overcome pornography and sexual sin?

 *Take a moment and reread these key sentences, then journal what they mean to you.*

1. Pornography, sexual sin, and sexual addiction are not just men's issues. Many women inside and outside of the church are entangled in this trap.

2. You are not alone.

3. Just because pornography and sexual sin are issues in your life today doesn't mean that they need to control your tomorrow. Through the work that Jesus did at the cross, there is always hope.

4. The same Jesus that changed the life of the woman at the well wants to lift every woman who is caught in sexual sin out of their shame and give them a new life. Through the work that Jesus did at the cross, anyone can break the cycle, overcome whatever has you bound, and win the battle over sexual sin.

5. You have hope. Hope that you can be free. Hope that you can overcome. Hope that just because it seems like this sin controls your heart and mind and it's impossible to break free, that nothing is impossible with God. (Matthew 19:26)

 ## Scriptures to focus on and memorize...

Can anything ever separate us from Christ's love? Does it mean he no longer loves us if we have trouble or calamity, or are persecuted, or hungry, or destitute, or in danger, or threatened with death? (As the Scriptures say, "For your sake we are killed every day; we are being slaughtered like sheep.")

No, despite all these things, overwhelming victory is ours through Christ, who loved us. -Romans 8:35-37 (NLT)

There is more joy in heaven over one lost sinner who repents and returns to God than over ninety-nine others who are righteous and haven't strayed away! -Luke 15:7 (NLT)

Chapter Two
Is God Against Sex?

"Then neither do I condemn you," Jesus declared. "Go now and leave your life of sin."

These were the words that Jesus spoke to the woman who was caught in adultery in John 8:11.

> *At dawn he appeared again in the temple courts, where all the people gathered around him, and he sat down to teach them.*
>
> *The teachers of the law and the Pharisees brought in a woman caught in adultery. They made her stand before the group and said to Jesus,*
>
> *"Teacher, this woman was caught in the act of adultery. In the Law Moses commanded us to stone such women. Now what do you say?"*
>
> *They were using this question as a trap, in order to have a basis for accusing him.*

> *But Jesus bent down and started to write on the ground with his finger. When they kept on questioning him, he straightened up and said to them, "Let any one of you who is without sin be the first to throw a stone at her."*
>
> *Again he stooped down and wrote on the ground. At this, those who heard began to go away one at a time, the older ones first, until only Jesus was left, with the woman still standing there.*
>
> *Jesus straightened up and asked her, "Woman, where are they? Has no one condemned you?"*
>
> *"No one, sir," she said.*
>
> *"Then neither do I condemn you," Jesus declared. "Go now and leave your life of sin." -John 8:1-11 (NIV)*

They were in the Temple. The religious leaders knew the Law, and they had skillfully planned a scheme to trap Jesus using it. She meant nothing to them. She was just a pawn in their scheme—the bait used to set the trap. They honestly didn't care what happened to her–it was all about their power and careers.

The whole scene was designed to trap Jesus between Jewish Law, which said that in very specific circumstances, adultery was punishable by execution (Deuteronomy 22:23-24), and Roman law, which did not allow Jews to carry out death sentences.

Jesus knew this. Cleverly, Jesus gave them the perfect answer. He shifted the burden of the decision to them when He said, **"Let any one of you who is without sin be the first to throw a stone at her."** One by one, they were forced to lay down their rocks and walk away. Instead of looking at what SHE had done, they had to look at what THEY had done.

After her accusers dispersed, the woman was left alone with Jesus.

Is God Against Sex?

I can't imagine what she was thinking. I'm sure she was afraid. I mean, what the religious leaders did was pretty traumatic. I'm sure she was humiliated—having her secret sin exposed to everyone in the public square. I wonder if there wasn't also a part of her that was amazed.

Who was this man Who saved her life?

And why did He do it? Let's be honest: Even though we don't know all of the details involved in her affair, and we don't know why they didn't drag the man with whom she was having an affair out to be stoned—the fact was that she was guilty. According to Jewish Law, she could have been stoned.

Why did He save her? Now that they were alone, what would happen next?

She didn't have to wait long for an answer. His response to this woman demonstrates the heart of God toward every person who is trapped in sexual sin: ***"Then neither do I condemn you," Jesus declared. "Go now and leave your life of sin."***

Can you imagine her surprise when she heard His words and realized that Jesus—the only One in the crowd Who had never sinned and had every right to throw a stone—didn't want to see her punished and die for her sin?

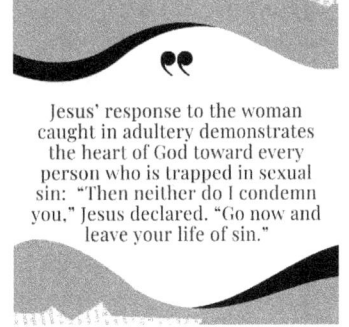

Jesus' response to the woman caught in adultery demonstrates the heart of God toward every person who is trapped in sexual sin: "Then neither do I condemn you," Jesus declared. "Go now and leave your life of sin."

Instead, He offered her grace.

Mercy.

He literally said, *"I don't condemn you."* He spoke kindly to her and offered her forgiveness.

This is still God's heart for every woman trapped in sexual sin. He doesn't want to humiliate, embarrass, or expose you to shame. He doesn't want to punish you for your sin. That's not God's heart and undoubtedly not His character.

Instead, God is merciful.

> *The Lord is compassionate and merciful, slow to get anger and filled with unfailing love. -Psalm 103:8 (NIV)*
>
> *All of us also lived among them at one time, gratifying the cravings of our flesh and following its desires and thoughts. Like the rest, we were by nature deserving of wrath.*
>
> *But because of his great love for us, God, who is rich in mercy, made us alive with Christ even when we were dead in transgressions—it is by grace you have been saved. -Ephesians 2:3-5 (NIV)*

The Greek word here for "mercy" is "eleos," which means "mercy, pity; the moral quality of feeling compassion and especially of showing kindness toward someone in need. This can refer to a human kindness and to God's kindness to humankind"[1]

God is also gracious.

> *The Lord is merciful and gracious, slow to anger and abounding in steadfast love. He will not always chide, nor will he keep his anger forever.*
>
> *He does not deal with us according to our sins nor repay us according to our iniquities.*
>
> *For as high as the heavens are above the earth, so great is his steadfast love toward those who fear him; as far as the east is from the west, so far does he remove our transgressions from us.*

> *As a father shows compassion to his children, so the Lord shows compassion to those who fear him. For he knows our frame; he remembers that we are dust.* -Psalm 103:8-14 (ESV)

"These two character traits: grace and mercy represent two aspects of God's character. To experience the grace of God is to receive a gift that one cannot earn and does not deserve.

To experience the mercy of God is to be preserved from punishment that one does in fact deserve....When God forgives our sin and guilt, we are experiencing mercy. When we receive the gift of life, we are experiencing grace. God's mercy removes the punishment, while His grace replaces the negative with a positive."[2]

Here is another important character trait of God: He is love. (1 John 4:8) Think about that—it doesn't just mean that God loves (using love as a verb) but that God is love (a noun).

1 John 4:9-10 shows us that God's loving character is displayed through the sacrifice of His Son for our redemption.

> *This is how God showed his love for us: God sent his only Son into the world so we might live through him. This is the kind of love we are talking about—not that we once upon a time loved God, but that he loved us and sent his Son as a sacrifice to clear away our sins and the damage they've done to our relationship with God.* (Message)

The truth is that it never has been and never will be God's desire that anyone suffer and die for their sins. God doesn't want people to be punished, and He doesn't want them to go to Hell. Instead, 2 Peter 3:9 tells us that God wants everyone to repent.

> *The Lord is not slow in keeping his promise, as some understand slowness. Instead he is patient with you, not wanting anyone to perish, but everyone to come to*

repentance. (NIV)

This is why God sent Jesus into the world—to pay the price for all of our sins.

> *For this is how God loved the world: He gave his one and only Son, so that everyone who believes in him will not perish but have eternal life. God sent his Son into the world not to judge the world, but to save the world through him. -John 3:16-17 (NLT)*

That is what is amazing about God's grace. Even though we sinned and rebelled against His ways, breaking the relationship between man and God, God did all the work of bringing restoration, forgiveness, and healing.

> Because of His character, when you come to Jesus and confess your sin, He is not waiting to pounce and punish. Instead, like the father in the story of the prodigal son, God is waiting with loving and open arms to forgive you and extend His grace to you.

He doesn't want sin to destroy our lives. He wants us to have an abundant life centered on our relationship with Him and experiencing the benefits of living within His Law.

God's grace, His mercy, His love, and His forgiveness provide hope for every woman who wants to be free from their sexual sin. Because of His character, when you come to Jesus and confess your sin, He is not waiting to pounce and punish. Instead, like the father in the story of the prodigal son, God is waiting with loving and open arms to forgive you and extend His grace to you.

> *So then, since we have a great High Priest who has entered heaven, Jesus the Son of God, let us hold firmly to what we believe. This High Priest of ours understands our weaknesses, for he faced all of the same testings we do, yet he did not sin.*

Is God Against Sex?

So let us come boldly to the throne of our gracious God. There we will receive his mercy, and we will find grace to help us when we need it most. -Hebrews 4:14-16 (NLT)

Like Jesus did with the woman caught in adultery, Jesus wants to give you grace and mercy, not condemnation. However, just as Jesus' conversation with the woman caught in adultery didn't end there, Jesus also has more for you.

Just like the woman caught in adultery, Jesus also wants to give you a new life free from the sin that holds you in bondage. Even though God did everything He could to offer you forgiveness of sin, grace, and mercy, the new life that God wants you to have only *happens as you partner with God and "Go and sin no more."*

Even though God did everything He could to offer you forgiveness of sin, grace, and mercy, the new life that God wants you to have only happens as you partner with God and "Go and sin no more."

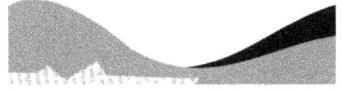

This is the part that many in today's culture and Progressive Christianity want to ignore. They like the part where God is loving, merciful, and gracious. They even twist the Scriptures and misinterpret them, saying, *"Because God loves me, He wants me to be happy. If a behavior (particularly sexual sin) makes me happy, then God does not have a problem with it."* Using this logic, they teach that there is no such thing as sexual sin.

One popular progressive teacher even goes so far as to teach that it was God's will that she abandoned her husband and children and married a woman. After all, God wants her to be happy and fulfilled, and this is what brings her joy.[3]

Obviously, this is not good theology.

The truth is that God loves you and wants to see you live a full, abundant life. That is why, throughout Scripture, He gave His people moral laws, knowing that these boundaries would ultimately be for their health, their benefit, and their enjoyment. Because God knows everything, He knows that even though sexual sin might bring momentary pleasure, in the end, living outside of His boundaries would result in heartache, trauma, and chaos. Because of His love, He gave us boundaries.

That's why it is essential that we embrace both sides of Jesus' conversation with the woman caught in adultery. As incredible as God's grace and mercy are, it is also God's will that we choose to do whatever is necessary to abandon our sexual sin, and choose to live according to God's plan for our sexuality.

This brings us to the following question: **What does the Bible say about sex?**

The Bible says that God created sex to be enjoyed by one man and one woman within the marriage covenant. Anything else is a sin.

As the Scriptures say, *"A man leaves his father and mother and is joined to his wife, and the two are united into one."* *-Ephesians 5:31 (NLT)*

The first marriage and the first sexual encounter took place in Genesis between Adam and Eve. For all the critics who say, *"God and the church are just against sex,"* this is proof that sex was God's idea, and He intended it to be enjoyed. It premieres in the first few chapters of Genesis, and it's built into the creation story.

In God's plan, sex also had a purpose. Sex was intended to create intimacy and deepen the relationship between a husband and wife, as well as for pleasure and procreation.

The problem is that in Genesis 3, sin entered the world. Over time, people began abandoning God's plan for sex within marriage and began perverting it. It isn't long before we see adultery, fornication, polygamy, rape, incest, prostitution, and homosexuality recorded in the Old Testament. Another thing you'll see as you study the Old Testament is that the nations who worshipped idols included disgusting sexual perversion and human sacrifice in their religious rituals.

This is why when God set up His Law for His people to follow, He made it clear that they were not to follow the customs of the people around them. The Israelites were not to worship their idols, and they were not to follow their customs. Instead, God wanted His people to be a reflection of His holiness. He wanted them to live in a way that would reflect His original purpose when He created humanity—that men and women would have a personal relationship with Him and healthy relationships with each other.

That's why God's Laws included so many specifics regarding sexuality. Ultimately, because He knew that it was best for men, women, and families, God wanted His people to live by His original plan—sex was to be enjoyed by a husband and wife within marriage.

Because God knew what was best for men, women, and families, God wanted His people to live by His original plan...Sex was to be enjoyed by a husband and wife within marriage.

This is where many who want to say that the Bible is an antiquated document filled with Laws that don't apply today will ask, *"But that's the Old Testament. Didn't Jesus set us free from those Laws?"*

Well, yes and no.

When Jesus died on the cross, He fulfilled all of the requirements of the Old Testament Laws. This means that because of Jesus' work at the cross, we no longer have to live under the ceremonial laws of Moses. We don't have to sacrifice lambs or bulls or have a high priest make atonement for our sins once a year. Jesus took care of all of that at the cross. He also did away with the civil law—the law that applied specifically to the Jewish people living at that time. This means we don't have to worry about the laws about planting two seeds in a field, mixing two types of fabric (which is fantastic because I love me some spandex in my jeans) or what to do if one bull gores another. As Paul makes clear throughout the New Testament, these Old Testament Laws no longer apply to us.

However, there is a set of Laws that have never changed and will never change. These are God's moral laws. They reflect God's character and show how He wants His people to live.

How do we know if something is a moral law?

The simple answer is that it is repeated in the New Testament. Have no doubt—the New Testament has a lot to say about abstaining from sexual sin. It's so important that when they held the Council at Jerusalem to answer the question of what Old Testament Laws the Gentile believers had to follow and which they could ignore, the answer said:

> *"And so my judgment is that we should not make it difficult for the Gentiles who are turning to God. Instead, we should write and tell them to abstain from eating food offered to idols,*
>
> *from sexual immorality,*
>
> *from eating the meat of strangled animals, and from consuming blood. For these laws of Moses have been preached in Jewish synagogues in every city on every Sabbath for many generations." -Acts 15:19-21 (NLT)*

As we read through the New Testament, we see that almost every book discusses the need for followers of Christ to overcome and avoid sexual sin.

Here are some examples:

• 1 Corinthians 6:9 says that fornication (sex outside of marriage between unmarried people) is a sin. This includes living together before marriage. There's no age limit or excuse. If you aren't married, you shouldn't be having sex.

> ***Know ye not that the unrighteous shall not inherit the kingdom of God? Be not deceived: neither fornicators, nor idolaters, nor adulterers, nor effeminate, nor abusers of themselves with mankind, (KJV)***

• Hebrews 13:4 teaches that adultery (having sex with someone else's marriage partner) is sin.

• 1 Timothy 1:10 says homosexuality is a sin.

• I Peter 4:3 teaches that orgies and drunken debauchery is a sin. (This would include getting drunk and having a one-night stand.)

• 1 Thessalonians 4:3-8 teaches that it is God's will that we be sanctified and avoid sexual immorality. These verses say that anyone who rejects this teaching is rejecting God.

• Galatians 5:19-21 explicitly says that anyone who is having sex outside of marriage will not inherit the kingdom of God.

At this point, some may be thinking, *"Whew, the New Testament doesn't say anything about pornography. I guess God doesn't think that's a big deal. Besides, looking at pornography isn't really sex, is it?"*

Wait, not so fast. To find the New Testament perspective on pornography, we need to look at what Jesus says in Matthew 5:27-28:

> ***You have heard that it was said, 'You shall not commit adultery.' But I tell you that anyone who looks at a woman with lustful intent has already committed adultery with her in his heart. (ESV)***

In God's eyes, pornography is the same as having sex; it says so right there. Sex is meant for the marriage bed, not in front of a computer, television, phone screen, or romance novel.

Jesus makes it clear. If we look at someone lustfully, we fantasize about someone, or if we use the highlight reel, it is a sin against God. There is no way around it.

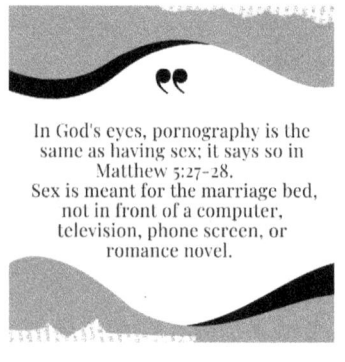

In God's eyes, pornography is the same as having sex; it says so in Matthew 5:27-28.
Sex is meant for the marriage bed, not in front of a computer, television, phone screen, or romance novel.

Hence, the Bible is literally telling us to flee from pornography...this includes anything that focuses on the sensual, sexual, or arouses ungodly desires inside of us.

Philippians 4:8 says that we need to do more than keep our actions pure; we should focus on keeping our thoughts pure.

Please understand that we're not looking at these Scriptures to make you feel ashamed or defeated. Remember, God's character is not to cause shame. However, the Holy Spirit and God's Word do cause conviction as we see how God intended for us to function sexually and what behaviors are sinful.

When there are any areas in which we fall short of God's standard, we recognize this is a sin. That's when, like the woman caught in adultery, we can come to Jesus, repent, and ask for God's mercy, grace, and forgiveness, as well as God's help to go and sin no more.

In the next few chapters, we will focus on specific steps and tools that will help you *"go and sin no more."* However, as we wrap up this chapter, I encourage you to spend some time with Jesus.

Go back and read through the Scriptures about His love, mercy, and grace, and remember that He wants to forgive you for any and all sexual sins you are committing. He wants to help you overcome and have a healthy relationship and embrace healthy, holy sexuality.

Then, spend some time in prayer, thanking God for the gift of His grace, mercy, and love. Finish by asking Him to give you all the strength, courage, and Holy Spirit power to move forward and take the next steps as you determine to ***"go and sin no more."***

Group Study Questions...

1. What does the story of the woman caught in adultery teach us about God's heart toward women who are trapped in sexual sin?

2. This chapter discussed several character traits of God. What are they?

3. What is the difference between *"mercy"* and *"grace"*?

4. How did God do everything necessary to provide us with forgiveness of sins, grace, and mercy?

5. After reading this chapter, how would you answer the question, *"What does the Bible say about sex?"*

6. Does it surprise you that almost every book in the New Testament discusses the need for followers of Christ to overcome and avoid sexual sin?

7. How do you feel about Jesus' teaching in Matthew 5:27-28 which says that in God's eyes, pornography is the same as having sex?

8. After reading this chapter, what have you learned about God's heart revealed in the verse, ***"Then neither do I condemn you," Jesus declared. "Go now and leave your life of sin."***?

Questions to Answer Privately....

1. How did you feel reading the story of the woman caught in adultery?

2. How do you think she felt as it was happening? How do you think she felt about Jesus' words?

3. Do you see God as compassionate, loving, merciful, and gracious, or do you see Him waiting to pounce and punish you for your sins?

4. Have you been influenced by the false teaching of popular Progressive Christian teachers who say that God prioritizes your happiness over your purity? After reading this chapter, can you see how this is false teaching?

5. What sexual sins do you participate in that are against Biblical teaching? Be specific.

6. Will you go to God and ask Him to forgive you of those sins so that you can experience His grace and mercy?

7. After spending time in prayer asking the Holy Spirit for help and guidance, write out a plan to help you to *"go and sin no more."*

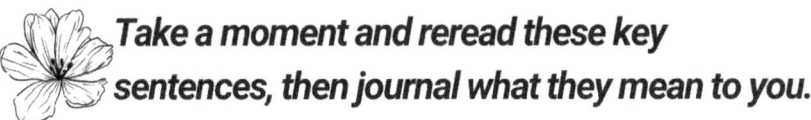 *Take a moment and reread these key sentences, then journal what they mean to you.*

1. Because of His character, when you come to Jesus and confess your sin, He is not waiting to pounce and punish. Instead, like the father in the story of the prodigal son, God is waiting with loving and open arms to forgive you and extend His grace to you.

2. God's original purpose when He created humans was for men and women to have a personal relationship with Him and healthy relationships with each other.

3. Almost every book in the New Testament discusses the need for followers of Christ to overcome and avoid sexual sin.

4. In God's eyes, pornography is the same as having sex. Jesus makes it clear. If we look at someone lustfully, we fantasize about someone, or if we use the highlight reel, it is a sin against God. There is no way around it.

5. God's character is not to cause shame. However, the Holy Spirit and God's Word do cause conviction as we see how God intended for us to function sexually and what behaviors are sinful.

Is God Against Sex?

 ## Scriptures to focus on and memorize...

"Then neither do I condemn you," Jesus declared. "Go now and leave your life of sin." -John 8:11 (NIV)

The Lord is not slow in keeping his promise, as some understand slowness. Instead he is patient with you, not wanting anyone to perish, but everyone to come to repentance. -2 Peter 3:9 (NIV)

Marriage should be honored by all, and the marriage bed kept pure, for God will judge the adulterer and all the sexually immoral.-Hebrews 13:4, (NIV)

For you have spent enough time in the past doing what pagans choose to do—living in debauchery, lust, drunkenness, orgies, carousing and detestable idolatry. -1 Peter 4:3 (NIV)

You say, "Food for the stomach and the stomach for food, and God will destroy them both." The body, however, is not meant for sexual immorality but for the Lord, and the Lord for the body.

By his power God raised the Lord from the dead, and he will raise us also. Do you not know that your bodies are members of Christ himself? Shall I then take the members of Christ and unite them with a prostitute? Never!

Do you not know that he who unites himself with a prostitute is one with her in body? For it is said, "The two will become one flesh." But whoever is united with the Lord is one with him in spirit.

Flee from sexual immorality. All other sins a person commits are outside the body, but whoever sins sexually, sins against their own body.

Do you not know that your bodies are temples of the Holy Spirit, who is in you, whom you have received from God? You are not your own; you were bought at a price. Therefore honor God with your bodies. -1 Corinthians 6:13-20 (NIV)

The acts of the flesh are obvious: sexual immorality, impurity and debauchery; idolatry and witchcraft; hatred, discord, jealousy, fits of rage, selfish ambition, dissensions, factions and envy; drunkenness, orgies, and the like. I warn you, as I did before, that those who live like this will not inherit the kingdom of God.

But the fruit of the Spirit is love, joy, peace, forbearance, kindness, goodness, faithfulness, gentleness and self-control. Against such things there is no law.

Those who belong to Christ Jesus have crucified the flesh with its passions and desires. Since we live by the Spirit, let us keep in step with the Spirit. Let us not become conceited, provoking and envying each other. -Galatians 5:19-26 (NIV)

Chapter Three
Coming Out Of The Dark

Several years ago, my brother and I were at a retreat with our board of directors. Two of our board members brought their kids, who were three and four years old, to the retreat. It was so much fun.

One of my favorite memories from the trip happened just after we all went to bed. Just as my head hit the pillow, I heard two little voices crying from across the hall, *"I can't sleep like this; it's too dark in here!"*

Honestly, there was a part of me that agreed. It was dark, and I was missing the night light I had at home.

The little ones and I were happy when their parents turned on the hall light, illuminating the dark, scary shadows. Just a little bit of light made all the difference.

One of the reasons that sexual sin can form such a powerful hold in a person's life is that it is often a hidden sin. Secrets sins thrive in darkness.

Often, because sexual sin carries shame, we don't discuss it. As we talked about in the first chapter, women can feel a sense of shame because pornography and sexual temptation are supposed to be masculine problems. Often, women keep their sins hidden because they worry about what people will think of them if they find out.

Then there are the potential consequences: if the secret sin is uncovered, you could lose your marriage, your family, or your reputation. With such tremendous potential consequences, most who struggle with this sin keep it hidden.

That's the problem with hidden sins—they thrive on darkness and secrets. It's like fertilizer to a plant. The more you keep your sin hidden away, the deeper the roots of the sin grow until it completely controls your life.

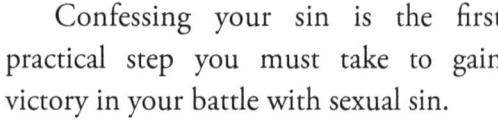

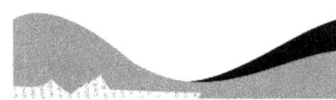

Confessing your sins is the best weapon in defeating hidden sins in your life.

That's why confessing your sins is the best weapon in defeating hidden sins in your life. If you want freedom, you must shine a big old light on it.

Confessing your sin is the first practical step you must take to gain victory in your battle with sexual sin.

This begins with **confessing** *our sins to is God.*

1 John 1:9 says, "But if we confess our sins to him, he is faithful and just to forgive us our sins and to cleanse us from all wickedness." (NLT)

One person who sets an excellent example of how we can repent after we have fallen into sexual sin is King David.

His story begins in 2 Samuel 11:1-5:

In the spring of the year, when kings normally go out to

war, David sent Joab and the Israelite army to fight the Ammonites. They destroyed the Ammonite army and laid siege to the city of Rabbah. However, David stayed behind in Jerusalem.

Late one afternoon, after his midday rest, David got out of bed and was walking on the roof of the palace. As he looked out over the city, he noticed a woman of unusual beauty taking a bath.

He sent someone to find out who she was, and he was told, "She is Bathsheba, the daughter of Eliam and the wife of Uriah the Hittite."

Then David sent messengers to get her; and when she came to the palace, he slept with her. She had just completed the purification rites after having her menstrual period. Then she returned home. (NLT)

The great King David, the slayer of giants, the man after God's own heart, had sinned. His lustful eyes caused him to sin. When Bathsheba became pregnant, he killed her husband to cover it up. (2 Samuel 11:6-27)

The leader of Israel broke two of the Ten Commandments. **"You shall not murder. You shall not commit adultery." (Exodus 20:13-14)**

Although David hoped that no one would ever discover his secret, God knew, and He wasn't pleased.

In 2 Samuel 12, we see that God sent Nathan, the prophet, to confront David with his sin.

Presented with his sin, David didn't try to deny it or make excuses. Instead, he said, **"I have sinned against the Lord." -2 Samuel 12:13, (NLT)**

WHATEVER IS LOVELY

David recognized that his sin was a big deal. He acknowledged, as Joseph said in Genesis 39:9, that all sexual sin is sin against God, and he wholeheartedly and thoroughly repented.

Psalm 51 is the exact words that David prayed after he faced his sin. In this psalm, we see some of the attitudes necessary to thoroughly repent of our sins and overcome sexual sin.

- First, David thoroughly confessed his sin. (Psalm 51:1-6)

- Next, David asked God to forgive him and cleanse him of all unrighteousness. (Psalm 51:7-11)

- Finally, David desires to stop sinning and live by God's ways. (Psalm 51:12-19)

This last point is such an essential part of repentance and overcoming sexual sin: **you do everything possible to get that sin out of your life and live differently.**

The best way to deal a blow to the enemy is to be specific when you go before God and repent of any and all sexual sins you have committed in the past.

You take a sledgehammer to it and destroy it. You demolish it. You do whatever is necessary—whatever you must do to get the sin and any stronghold it has formed out of your life.

One practice that will help you do this is to go beyond just asking God to forgive you for generalized sexual sin. The best way to deal a blow to the enemy is to be specific when you go before God and repent of any and all sexual sins you have committed in the past.

This is something that I did over twenty-five years ago after I got caught in the trap of watching far too much soft pornography on television and in movies. I also read too much graphic content in fictional novels and women's magazines. Like always happens when you give pornography even a foothold, it created an appetite in my life.

After I came home from college, God was doing a lot of work in our family, revealing lies and abuse that were hidden throughout our lives. One day, while I was in my room praying, I felt the Holy Spirit's conviction so strongly for my secret sin. Completely broken, I knew this was the day I needed to deal with this issue once and for all.

One of the things I did to gain freedom completely was to take a sheet of paper (it was a long time ago—we didn't have computers), and I wrote down every single time I watched a television show or movie that was sexually explicit. I wrote down every romance novel or magazine I read with sexually explicit content. As the Holy Spirit brought things to my mind, I listed inappropriate music I was listening to, and then I went through each item and asked God to forgive me. All in all, it was a pretty long list.

Then, I spent time in prayer, confessing each individual sin to God. I asked Him to forgive me and restore my mind to purity and holiness like His.

Is this an extreme measure?

Yes.

But I was extremely serious about overcoming this sin and conquering it once and for all.

As the lists were made, I confessed sins and saw patterns develop.

- When did I fall into these sins?
- What was happening?
- What were the triggers and the causes?

WHATEVER IS LOVELY

- Were there other areas that I needed to overcome?

Even though this practice may seem a little old-fashioned, it helped me thoroughly confess my sin and see what needed to change in my life.

True repentance doesn't end with just saying "sorry." True repentance means that you change.

Because true repentance doesn't end with just saying *"sorry."* True repentance means that you change. No, change isn't always easy, but true repentance does whatever it takes to change your behavior—to stop sinning. Repentance means turning around and going in the opposite direction.

Here's the amazing part: *when you decide to do everything you can to remove sin from your life, the Holy Spirit inside you partners with you to give you the strength to do everything you can't do on your own.*

When your continued determination partners with the power of the Holy Spirit, together you can overcome any sin, restore your relationship with God, and do the work necessary to fix your relationship with others and your reputation.

The truth is that no woman is too broken to experience God's forgiveness and healing and start a new life. But the key is to humble yourself before God in repentance, ask for forgiveness, and partner with the Holy Spirit to stop sinning.

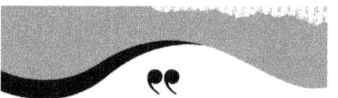

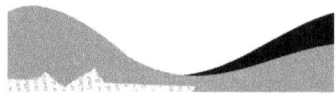

No woman is too broken to experience God's forgiveness and healing and start a new life.

To admit, like David did, I have sinned, but I don't want this to be the end of my story.

Another thing that will help you show that you are serious about change is **confessing your sin to someone else.** While it is only necessary to confess your sin to God to be forgiven, confessing to another person helps you bring your sin further out of the darkness and provide accountability.

> *Therefore confess your sins to each other and pray for each other so that you may be healed. The prayer of a righteous person is powerful and effective. -James 5:16 (NIV)*

Accountability breaks the stranglehold secrets and shame have on your life. Stop keeping it a secret. You need to tell someone.

Looking back on my personal struggle to overcome this issue over twenty-five years ago, I can testify that my accountability partner kept me on the straight and narrow. As I said, I was living with my parents at the time. The same day that I fell under the Holy Spirit's conviction, I confessed my sin to my Mom.

It wasn't easy at all. Here's the thing—she was very compassionate and understanding on the day I repented. She showed me God's grace and compassion and encouraged me that she loved me and believed I could overcome.

However (and this is a BIG "however"), my Mom was a tough accountability partner. Now, understand, I wanted to overcome this. I gave her permission to ask me any questions, and I wanted her to hold me accountable.

And she did.

Her questions were direct, invasive, and not always easy to answer.

But that is precisely what I needed because whenever I was tempted to fall back into old patterns, one of the things that helped me resist temptation was knowing that I'd have to tell my Mom. There was no way I wanted to do that! I couldn't face her disappointment, which helped me fight harder to resist temptation.

I know from experience that accountability is the best weapon in your fight against sexual sin. Just like the light of the sun kills germs and bacteria, shining a light on sin helps you overcome it. Giving someone else permission to shine a light in your life really helps you do all you can to fight against sin.

Now, obviously, you can't tell just anyone. That would be very unwise. We know that you can't tell everything to everyone. Some people are untrustworthy and will tell your secrets to anyone who will listen. Some people will use what we tell them to hurt us.

Don't talk to people who have this reputation. Avoid gossips, busybodies, or people who seem to know everything about everybody.

However, you can't let bad apples ruin the whole bunch. Don't let the fear of gossip keep you from finding the genuinely godly people willing to listen and help you through your issues.

Here are some things to look for in an accountability partner:

- Make sure they are a born-again Christian who believes that the Bible is God's Word.

- Look for someone who has been saved for a few years and is growing and maturing in their faith.

- When it comes to the topic of sexual sin, it is best to speak to someone of the same gender. Women talk to women, and men talk to men.

- Make sure they are trustworthy and can keep a secret.

Here's the thing: even though you need to be wise, it is absolutely essential that you find a trustworthy, godly woman with whom you can share your secrets and who will hold you accountable as you move forward in your fight to overcome.

You need to permit them to ask you direct questions like:

"When was the last time you looked at pornography or watched something on television or a movie that was sexually explicit?"

You might even want to tell them exactly how you are struggling so they can be specific and say, *"Did you watch this show this week? What books are you reading? Do you go on this website?"*

Let them ask you about your thought life and say, *"Are you struggling with lust?"*

"When was the last time you had contact with that man who isn't your husband?"

"When was the last time you felt tempted to fall back into your old ways?"

"What did you do when you felt temptation?"

Here's the thing: if we are going to overcome sexual sin, we need accountability. We need someone or several people around us who have total access to us, can ask us any questions, and can hold us accountable for anything they see fit. We need to be an open book to them, allowing no question or topic to be off-limits.

Here are some other suggestions for how to make the most of your relationship with your accountability partner:

1. Meet with them on a regular basis.

2. Give them access to your computer history.

3. Set aside time to pray with them and have them hold you accountable not just for your sexual life but for your devotional life.

Here is the most radical step that will help you win the battle against sexual sin:

Don't wait for them to ask you questions.

Whenever you feel tempted to fall back into sin, contact them and ask them to pray with you.

If you fall into old habits, confess your sin to your friend immediately.

I realize this sounds extreme, but knowing that if you sin, you must confess your sin to another person will help you resist temptation.

That is the goal—to go beyond just saying *"I'm sorry"* for your sin, but to truly repent and do whatever is necessary to overcome any ground you've given to sexual sin in your life.

I can't stress enough the importance of this step. I get it: The thought of revealing your hidden struggle can be terrifying, but don't let your fear keep you from freedom. When you shine a light on your hidden struggle, you will gain freedom and the ability to move forward in a life of purity.

 *Group Study Questions...*

1. What does it mean that secret sins thrive in darkness?

2. Read Genesis 39:9. How did Joseph's attitude about sexual sin help him flee temptation?

3. How does Psalm 51 demonstrate the attitudes necessary to repent of sexual sin thoroughly?

4. How do you feel about the statement: *"The best way to deal a blow to the enemy is to be specific when you go before God and repent of all sexual sins you have committed in the past."*?

5. How does the Holy Spirit partner with you to help you overcome sin?

6. What are the benefits of having an accountability partner?

 ## Questions to Answer Privately....

1. Have you confessed your sexual sin to God? If not, why are you avoiding it?

2. Make a list of every time you have sinned sexually, then take that list to God and thoroughly repent.

3. What did Psalm 51 and King David's repentance teach you personally about repenting of secret sin?

4. Do you have an accountability partner? If not, why?

5. List three people who could potentially be your accountability partner. Then, pray about which one to ask first.

6. Take a moment and create a plan for what you will say when you ask someone to be your accountability partner.

7. What specific areas do you need your accountability partner to hold you accountable? Are you willing to let your accountability partner ask you personal questions and answer them honestly without being offended?

8. Are you ready to do whatever it takes to be free from sexual sin—starting with bringing your secret out into the light?

> *Take a moment and reread these key sentences, then journal what they mean to you.*

1. That's the problem with hidden sins—they thrive on darkness and secrets. It's like fertilizer to a plant. The more you keep your sin hidden away, the deeper the roots of the sin grow until it completely controls your life.

2. The best way to deal a blow to the enemy is to be specific when you go before God and repent of any and all sexual sins you have committed in the past.

3. True repentance doesn't end with just saying *"sorry."* True repentance means that you change.

4. When you decide to do everything you can to remove sin from your life, the Holy Spirit inside you partners with you to give you the strength to do everything you can't do on your own.

 Scriptures to focus on and memorize...

But if we confess our sins to him, he is faithful and just to forgive us our sins and to cleanse us from all wickedness. -1 John 1:9 (NLT)

Finally, I confessed all my sins to you and stopped trying to hide my guilt.

I said to myself, "I will confess my rebellion to the Lord." And you forgave me! All my guilt is gone. -Psalm 32:5, (NLT)

People who conceal their sins will not prosper, but if they confess and turn from them, they will receive mercy. -Proverbs 28:13 (NLT)

My dear children, I am writing this to you so that you will not sin. But if anyone does sin, we have an advocate who pleads our case before the Father. He is Jesus Christ, the one who is truly righteous. He himself is the sacrifice that atones for our sins—and not only our sins but the sins of all the world. -1 John 2:1-2 (NLT)

Come close to God, and God will come close to you. Wash your hands, you sinners; purify your hearts, for your loyalty is divided between God and the world. Let there be tears for what you have done. Let there be sorrow and deep grief. Let there be sadness instead of laughter, and gloom instead of joy. Humble yourselves before the Lord, and he will lift you up in honor. -James 4:8-10 (NLT)

Chapter Four
Creating A Battle Plan

Now it's time to get practical. Until this point, we've talked about what the Bible says about sexual sin, God's grace and forgiveness, and our need to confess our sins to God and find an accountability partner. Far too often, people fall for the lie that this is all there is to winning the battle. They've confessed their sin, found an accountability partner, and put some accountability software on their phone, so like a magic formula, bing, bang, boom, the problem is solved.

Then, they are surprised when temptation comes back around and knocks them to the ground again. Disappointed and discouraged that the battle was more challenging than they thought, many start to believe they will never be free. They wonder, *"How did this happen? I did what I was supposed to do. Why am I still fighting this battle? Is it impossible for me to be free?"*

The answer to the last question is a resounding *"no."* Freedom is possible.

As we discussed in a previous chapter, when you make a firm decision to eradicate sin from your life, the Holy Spirit, Who resides within you, becomes your partner. He empowers you with the strength to overcome the challenges that you cannot face alone.

But here's the catch—you must do everything you can to fight.

It reminds me of Paul's words in Hebrews 12:2-4:

> *Therefore, since we are surrounded by so great a cloud of witnesses, let us also lay aside every weight, and sin which clings so closely, and let us run with endurance the race that is set before us,*
>
> *Looking to Jesus, the founder and perfecter of our faith, who for the joy that was set before him endured the cross, despising the shame, and is seated at the right hand of the throne of God.*
>
> *Consider him who endured from sinners such hostility against himself, so that you may not grow weary or fainthearted.*
>
> *In your struggle against sin you have not yet resisted to the point of shedding your blood. (ESV)*

In these verses, Paul challenges us to do all we can to overcome sin in our lives—especially the sins that *"so easily entangle us."* These are the ones that seem to come naturally to us and the ones we struggle the most to overcome. The *Fire Bible* says this literally refers to our most troublesome, sidetracking sins.[1] How many can agree that watching pornography can easily fall into this description?

The interesting thing here is that Paul doesn't say, *"If you feel like it,"* *"If you can get around to it,"* or *"Do the best you can,"* but Paul gets right to the point when he says, **"In your struggle against sin, you have not yet resisted to the point of shedding your blood."**

Can we take a moment and think about this?

Paul's message is clear: you can't just put a band-aid on sins like pornography or sexual temptation. Overcoming sin is not easy, but it's a fight you must be prepared to engage in continuously until you achieve full, complete, and total victory.

Another crucial point to remember in our struggle against sin is to never underestimate our enemy. Sin is a formidable adversary that requires our constant vigilance and determination.

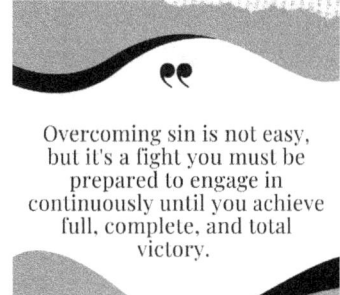

Overcoming sin is not easy, but it's a fight you must be prepared to engage in continuously until you achieve full, complete, and total victory.

1 Peter 5:8 says, ***"Stay alert! Watch out for your great enemy, the devil. He prowls around like a roaring lion, looking for someone to devour." (NLT)***

So here's some honest truth—are you ready for it?

Satan, your enemy, does not want you to gain victory over pornography and sexual sin.

He wants you to stay trapped in this sin so that it can destroy you. He doesn't want you to have a personal relationship with God, grow in your faith, become the woman God called you to be, and do all God called you to do.

Instead, as 1 Peter 5:8 says, Satan wants to devour you. He wants sin to come between you and God so that you are so covered in guilt and shame that you feel you can't go to God and have a personal relationship with Him.

Satan wants you to be so consumed with shame that you avoid reading God's Word and hearing it in church.

He wants to keep you bound in secrets and lies, avoiding other people so that no one will discover your secret.

Ultimately, he wants the sin that you have given a foothold to grow so entirely out of control in your life that it destroys you, your marriage, your family, all of your relationships, and your relationship with God and your witness for Him.

Here's another painful reality: **just because you took the first steps to freedom doesn't mean the enemy will give up his fight.**

It's like a scene from the sitcom *Young Sheldon*, where a nine-year-old Sheldon has locked himself in his garage and plans to live there forever to protect himself from germs. After trying to reason with him to no avail, his mother eventually gets frustrated, goes into the garage, and plans to carry him out.

As they chase each other around the garage, his mother, Mary, says, *"You can't run away from me forever."*

To which a sassy Sheldon replies, *"I don't have to do it forever…just until you get tired."* [2]

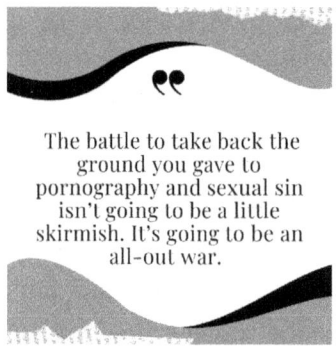

The battle to take back the ground you gave to pornography and sexual sin isn't going to be a little skirmish. It's going to be an all-out war.

And that, my friends, is why it's so hard to gain victory over pornography and sexual sin. Because, like Sheldon, Satan is waiting to see if you are really committed to fighting for your freedom or if you will eventually get tired of the fight, give up, allowing him to win.

So, how can anyone ever overcome?

You have to turn the tables, take on the attitude of Sheldon, and determine that you will be the last one standing.

You need to realize that the battle to take back the ground you gave to pornography and sexual sin isn't going to be a little skirmish.

Creating A Battle Plan

It's going to be an all-out war.

It's not going to be easy. It will take a lot of work, self-examination, sacrifice, and perseverance on your part. Deep inside your heart, you will need to determine that you want to be free and that you are going to do whatever it takes for as long as it takes you to gain your freedom.

Because that's what's necessary to win this battle.

Don't let these facts be a discouragement to you or make you feel hopeless. There is hope! Here is the good news—you can win the battle. Let's keep reading in 1 Peter 5 to find some encouragement:

> ***Stand firm against him, and be strong in your faith. Remember that your family of believers all over the world is going through the same kind of suffering you are.***
>
> ***In his kindness God called you to share in his eternal glory by means of Christ Jesus. So after you have suffered a little while, he will restore, support, and strengthen you, and he will place you on a firm foundation. -1 Peter 5:9-10, (NLT)***

Yes, the enemy wants to destroy you.

And yes, your freedom will only come as you are determined to fight, resist the enemy, and stand firm in the faith.

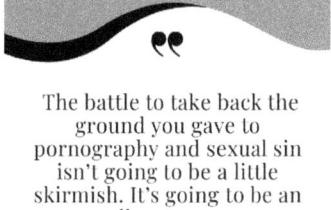

The battle to take back the ground you gave to pornography and sexual sin isn't going to be a little skirmish. It's going to be an all-out war.

But here's some hope:

First, you're not the only one going through these struggles. As we discussed in Chapter 1, many others are fighting and winning their battles and gaining victory in their lives.

More importantly, again, we see God's promise that as you fight, He will help and strengthen you, help you stand firm, hold your ground, and win the fight. As you do all you can do to stand against sin, God will empower you to help you overcome.

The question is, *"Are you ready to do all you can?"*

If your answer is *"yes,"* then it's time to start creating a battle plan. **The first step in creating a plan to overcome is to make an accurate assessment of your weaknesses. This starts with accessing your vulnerabilities.**

We need to realize when we are most vulnerable to falling into sexual sin so we can take steps to avoid it.

- Does loneliness cause you to sin?

- Do you watch pornography when you're bored and have nothing else to do?

- Do you tend to be tempted when you are under stress?

- Are you most vulnerable when you are tired?

- Does fighting with a family member or spouse lead you down this path?

- Does being isolated open you up to falling into this sin?

- Does sexual sin comfort you when you are experiencing trauma?

- Does sexual sin help console you when you remember childhood abuse?

These are just a few possibilities of times you may be vulnerable. Certainly, other circumstances or situations can cause you to feel the pull of temptation more strongly than others. The point is that you need to analyze yourself and discover:

Creating A Battle Plan

- What are you doing when you feel most tempted?
- What are your physical circumstances?
- What are your surroundings?

Here's an important question: **What are you feeling?**

Specifically, what emotions are you experiencing?

Are you sad, angry, disappointed, afraid, or anxious? You must identify what specific emotional need you are using sexual sin to fulfill.

Here's an example from a very popular television show that centers on a woman who carries a lot of baggage from her past. Most of the time, she's a competent, intelligent, quick-witted, charming person. She's strong and independent—the one others come to for help. Yet, there's another part of her that is still working through her issues with her parents and her childhood. While there are many parts of this character that I admire, her biggest flaw is that whenever someone or her parents hurt her or do something that wounds her deeply, she almost always turns to casual sex, which she later regrets, to find comfort.

Unfortunately, this fictional character reflects the lives of many women. Even inside the church, women know that their behavior is sinful and want to overcome it. They go to the altar and repent, but they keep falling back into the same cycle. One reason they keep falling for temptation is that they don't realize that they need to get to the root of the problem, identify the source of their pain, and follow the Biblical steps that allow God to heal their pain.

You see, often, sexual sin, including pornography, is really just the result of more profound pain. This pain could include trauma or maybe even abuse.

How do we discover the root of our problem?

You start by asking the Holy Spirit.

John 16:13 tells us that one of the roles the Holy Spirit can play in our lives is leading us into truth.

> *When the Spirit of truth comes, he will guide you into all truth.* -John 16:13, (NLT)

This includes helping us remember the things from our past that are causing pain in our hearts. This has happened to me so many times as I've been dealing with issues in my life.

As you do all you can do to stand against sin, God will empower you to help you overcome.

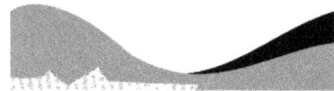

For instance, I remember when I asked the Holy Spirit to help me find the root cause of the anxiety that was devouring my life. Before long, the Holy Spirit began helping me remember moments from my childhood that I hadn't thought about in thirty or forty years. Sometimes, I'd remember things as I prayed; other times, the memories would resurface in dreams. Sometimes, while going about my day, I'd remember something. These memories showed me the root of the problem that needed to be healed so I could walk in freedom.

No matter how it happened, each time I asked the Holy Spirit to help me, He brought just the right memory to the surface in the right way and at the right time. Then, He was there to comfort me through the next step of feeling the pain of the memory, processing it, and finding complete healing for the issue that was causing me pain.

If, during your time of self-examination, you find that there is trauma, abuse, or pain in your heart causing you to fall into sexual sin or be tempted to sin, then I want to encourage you to start taking the

Creating A Battle Plan

steps necessary to deal with this pain. As I said, I've been through this journey myself, and I've laid out in detail all the steps I took to gain freedom and victory in my books *Finding Healing, Mind-Blowing Truths: Steps to Healing*, and *Mind-Blowing Truths: Demolishing The Strongholds In Your Mind*. Each of these books will help you identify the issues in your heart and mind and, more importantly, apply Biblical truth and find healing.

Another Bible study I recommend that will help you overcome the issues and pain of your past is *Victory's Journey* by my friend, Laverne Weber. *Victory's Journey* is a Women's Small Group Curriculum that reaches deep into the heart to bring hope, healing, and new beginnings. Using the principles of God's Word, each lesson is geared to follow a progression of healing that leads to victory and freedom. I have read through this entire curriculum, and I know that if you commit to reading the book and working through the curriculum, it will help you. You can also visit their website to find a small group near you.

For those who need help overcoming their issues, I recommend contacting *Beyond Survival Ministries*—specifically their *A Time to Heal Beyond Survival* option. This Biblically-based, Spirit-filled healing ministry offers in-person counseling or Zoom counseling for those who are further away. They can also connect you with a trained counselor or small group in your area. You can find their contact information at: ***atimetohealbeyondsurvival.org***. I highly recommend this Spirit-filled counseling center.

Another Christian ministry that has online counseling specifically designed to help people overcome an addiction to pornography and sexual sin is *Pure Life Ministries*.

Pure Life Ministries' "Create in Me a Pure Heart Program" says it can help you wherever sexual sin has taken you. It is a six-week program that includes audio or video counseling from home, with flexible counseling hours based on your schedule. Pricing and details are available at ***purelifeministries.org/struggling-women.*** I do not have personal experience with *Pure Life Ministries;* however, it is highly recommended by people that I trust.

Another counseling center that offer a Biblically-based counseling perspective to help you overcome sexual sin and pornography is: *Emerge Counseling Ministries* at ***emerge.org.***

Many Assembly of God churches, including my home church, Christian Life Assembly in Camp Hill, Pa, offer the *Celebrate Recovery* program. Individuals in *Celebrate Recovery* are letting down their walls and addressing crippling challenges in their lives. These issues include anger, codependency, pornography, grief, gambling, eating disorders, alcohol and drug addictions, compulsive and dysfunctional behaviors, and devastating hurts. *Celebrate Recovery* helps individuals find healing from anything that keeps them from living the life God meant for them to live.

Celebrate Recovery is a faith-based, Christ-centered, 12-step recovery program that focuses on how God can heal broken and hurting lives. It gets people on the road to recovery and keeps them there through teaching, accountability, service and outreach.

If you choose to go to another counselor, here are some tips to help you choose the right counselor for you:

1. Choose a born-again, Bible-believing, Spirit-filled counselor.

Psalm 1:1 says **"Blessed is the man who walks not in the counsel of the ungodly, nor stands in the paths of sinners, nor sits in the seat of the scornful; But his delight is in the law of the Lord, and in His law he meditates day and night." (NKJV)**

Because true health and freedom can only be found in the truth of God's Word, it is very important that you find a counselor who will give you advice and wisdom that comes from and agrees with the

Creating A Battle Plan

Word of God.

I remember being told about a woman who was struggling with issues of insecurity. Wanting to overcome this, she went to a very well-meaning counselor but not a Christian. Her counselor encouraged her to step outside of her comfort zone and become sexually active, believing this would help her overcome her inhibitions.

Taking her counselor's advice, the woman began living a sinful lifestyle that only resulted in more pain and frustration in her life. It wasn't until a godly friend helped her see that although her counselor meant well, the advice she'd received was totally wrong. Together, they found a godly counselor who then had to begin repairing the damage caused by the ungodly counselor's advice.

Friends, I honestly don't want to see this happen to you. The only way to prevent it is to find a counselor who loves Jesus, is committed to living a godly life based on Biblical principles, and teaches those principles to their clients.

The truth is that the Bible gives us all the answers we need to live a healthy, holy, abundant life in Jesus. A godly counselor will help you find those answers, but a counselor who doesn't know Jesus and doesn't believe in the Bible will lead you away from the answers you need and into empty ideas and philosophies.

2. Ask the godly people in your life for recommendations.

Ask your pastor if he can recommend someone. Many churches offer counseling as part of their ministry. If your church doesn't, ask your pastor to recommend a church that he trusts that does. A good pastor will not see this as competition; instead, they will understand that the body of Christ works together to help people.

Christian counseling centers are also available. Again, your pastor or the staff at your church may be able to recommend a center in your area.

Even if it's a Christian counseling center, read through its statement of beliefs. Call it and ask for references. Talk to a godly person you trust and see if they are trustworthy and reliable. Don't just go online and pick anyone. Instead, check them out.

3.   Pray about it.

Ask the Holy Spirit to lead you to the right counselor who will help you work through the pain and end the cycle once and for all.

4.   Don't believe the lie that counseling isn't necessary.

One of the biggest tools that the enemy will use to keep you from walking in health and freedom is the lie that counseling isn't needed. Just about the time you're ready to make the phone call and set up an appointment, thoughts will go through your mind like, *"Why are you being such a baby? This is not a big deal--- you're just being a drama queen. You can handle this on your own, you don't need to go to a counselor and waste the time and money."*

Please allow me to be blunt: These thoughts are lies!

Counseling is NOT a waste of time or money. It is an investment in your most important asset—your heart and mind. Freedom and healing are ALWAYS worth the investment!

It's part of doing whatever it takes to win your battle and find freedom.

What do you do if the root of your problem isn't trauma or abuse? What if your struggle with pornography is an appetite that grew from exposure to pornography or sexual sin?

You keep creating a battle plan by asking yourself what triggers temptation in your life.

Creating A Battle Plan

Ask yourself questions like:

- When was the first time I saw pornography?
- How old was I?
- When did I start noticing that I wanted to see more?

Analyze the list we suggested you make as you confessed your sins to God and notice if any patterns developed.

- What types of pornography attract you the most?
- Do you struggle with a specific television show?
- Are you looking at pornographic magazines or pornography on the internet?
- Are you tempted after watching movies?
- Are you watching Anime or playing inappropriate video games?

The possibilities for tempting stimuli are endless.

What's important is that you identify the areas that cause you the most temptation so you can create a game plan to start overcoming specific temptations.

Here are some questions I believe women specifically need to ask themselves:

- Do I have friends who encourage me to look at pornography, participate in sexually explicit conversations, watch inappropriate movies or television, or read inappropriate books or magazines?
- Are my friends sending me inappropriate or pornographic memes or videos?
- Are my friends encouraging me to participate in activities like

visiting strip clubs or attending bachelorette parties with strippers?

• Do my activities with my friends center around watching sexually explicit reality TV, or book clubs with sexual content?

The fact is that there is a ridiculous double standard when it comes to women's entertainment and men's entertainment. Too many activities that women call pornography and sin when men do them are called *"just a fun time with the girls"* when women do it. This is wrong.

Too many activities that women call pornography and sin when men do them are called "just a fun time with the girls" when women do it. This is wrong.

Sometimes, going to battle against pornography and sexual sin means that we have to determine which friends are leading us down the wrong path and then ask ourselves if those friendships are worth staying trapped in sexual sin.

Often, we must be honest with ourselves and admit that 1 Corinthians 15:33 was right when saying, **"Bad company corrupts good character." (NLT)**

Some questions you might want to ask yourself are:

• Do my friends encourage me to engage in sexual sin or sinful activities?

• How will my friends respond when I tell them I don't want to participate in these activities?

• Will they respect my wishes or try to change my mind?

• If they don't respect my commitment to following God and His standards for purity, am I willing to give them up as friends?

As we said at the beginning, fighting the battle to gain freedom from pornography and sexual temptation isn't going to be easy.

Creating A Battle Plan

It will require sacrifice, hard work, and determination. Still, victory can be achieved for those willing to fight with all their might.

You must ask yourself today, *"Am I willing to do whatever it takes to win the battle?"*

Are you willing to honestly examine your life and analyze your thoughts, emotions, and behaviors so that you can create a battle plan to gain victory?

If your answer is *"yes,"* I encourage you to start today. Spend time alone with God and pray, ***"Search me, O God, and know my heart; test me and know my anxious thoughts. Point out anything in me that offends you, and lead me along the path of everlasting life." -Psalm 139:23-24, (NLT)***

As you follow the Holy Spirit's leading and create a battle plan to shore up your weak, vulnerable areas, you can fight and win your battle. Freedom can be yours!

WHATEVER IS LOVELY

 *Group Study Questions...*

1. Read Hebrews 12:2-4. What does this passage tell us about doing everything we can to overcome sin?

2. What does the phrase *"Sins that so easily entangle us"* mean?

3. Why is it important to identify these troublesome, sidetracking sins and how they work in our lives?

4. What does it mean to *"never underestimate our enemy"*?

5. What does the scene described in *Young Sheldon* teach us about our battle with sexual sin and pornography?

6. Why is it necessary to create a battle plan?

7. Why is it important to examine the role our friends play in overcoming pornography and sexual sin?

Creating A Battle Plan

*Questions to Answer Privately....*

1. Have you ever tried to overcome pornography or sexual sin before and felt frustrated when simple fixes didn't work?

2. This chapter lists many questions that will help you accurately assess your weaknesses and vulnerabilities. If you haven't already, go back and answer each question as honestly as possible.

3. After answering all of these questions and anything the Holy Spirit brings to your mind, do you see a pattern emerging? What are the root causes of your issues with pornography and sexual sin?

4. How can this list help you create healthy fences and boundaries to overcome temptation?

5. Honestly answer this question: Do you need to seek counseling to overcome your sexual sin, trauma, or abuse?

6. Are you willing to do whatever it takes to win the battle?

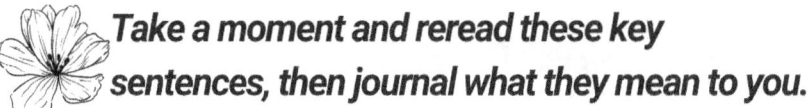 *Take a moment and reread these key sentences, then journal what they mean to you.*

1. You can't just put a band-aid on sins like pornography or sexual temptation. Overcoming sin is not easy, but it's a fight you must be prepared to engage in continuously until you achieve full, complete, and total victory.

2. The battle to take back the ground you gave to pornography and sexual sin isn't going to be a little skirmish. It's going to be an all-out war.

 Scriptures to focus on and memorize...

Stay alert! Watch out for your great enemy, the devil. He prowls around like a roaring lion, looking for someone to devour.

Stand firm against him, and be strong in your faith.

Remember that your family of believers all over the world is going through the same kind of suffering you are.

In his kindness God called you to share in his eternal glory by means of Christ Jesus. So after you have suffered a little while, he will restore, support, and strengthen you, and he will place you on a firm foundation. -1 Peter 5:8-10 (NLT)

Search me, O God, and know my heart; test me and know my anxious thoughts. Point out anything in me that offends you, and lead me along the path of everlasting life. -Psalm 139:23-24 (NLT)

So let's not get tired of doing what is good. At just the right time we will reap a harvest of blessing if we don't give up. -Galatians 6:9 (NLT)

Chapter Five
Tools To Help You Overcome

And now, dear brothers and sisters, one final thing. Fix your thoughts on what is true, and honorable, and right, and pure, and lovely, and admirable. Think about things that are excellent and worthy of praise. -Philippians 4:8 (NLT)

It's a popular Scripture. I can't tell you how many times I've heard or read it when someone is discussing purity. I've even written about it myself.

The question is, how do we practically obey this verse? In a world where we are constantly bombarded with sexual images and erotic messages, how do we focus on the pure, the noble, and the lovely?

Hitting even closer to home, how does someone who has struggled with pornography or sexual temptation turn the ship of their hearts away from focusing on sensual things and follow Paul's teaching in Philippians 4:8?

I believe it begins with defining two words: pornography and appetites.

According to Merriam-Webster, pornography is *"the depiction of erotic behavior (as in pictures or writing) intended to cause sexual excitement; the depiction of acts in a sensational manner so as to arouse a quick, intense emotional reaction."* [1]

That's a broad definition and covers more than how we usually define this word. Yet, our perspective changes when we accurately define pornography as any picture or writing that causes sexual excitement or that arouses a quick, intense emotional reaction.

This includes forms of *"soft"* pornography that many, including many Christian women, don't recognize as dangerous because they watch it on television, see it in movies, read it in romance novels, or view it on social media. After all, this isn't real pornography.

Still, it is a sin! These mediums are especially dangerous for women because when we get into the storyline, we tend to become emotionally involved. We laugh at the heroine's blunders and cry as they endure their struggles. We watch the romance grow between characters and want to see when they finally realize they are in love. Then, because we want to see the end of the story, we ignore the fact that their romance ends in the bedroom instead of the marriage altar and watch a steamy sex scene that falls right into the dictionary definition of pornography.

The more we watch scenes like this, the more we become desensitized, and our appetite grows until it becomes an addiction.

What do we mean by *"appetite"*?

An appetite is a feeling of wanting or needing something.[2] It's a craving inside the soul that has never been satisfied. It is striving after or towards something. It is something yearned for or longed for that

Tools To Help You Overcome

is never filled or satisfied. We use a variety of things and ways to fill this craving.

Appetites operate from our soul, the seat of our emotions, then through the heart and mind. They consume as much of the mind as they can. We want and want, but nothing satisfies.

Here's why it's important that we understand what these two words mean: From the first moment that we see any pornography, it creates an appetite inside of us to see more. Every time we feed this appetite, our hunger for pornography increases. This is why it often forms an addiction as our soul cries out, *"I want this, I need this, I enjoyed that, feed me now."*

From the first moment that we see any pornography, it creates an appetite inside of us to see more. Every time we feed this appetite, our hunger for pornography increases.

Even when we give in to hunger and the desire is momentarily met, it isn't long until we crave more. It's a powerful and insatiable appetite that ultimately controls and consumes people's lives.

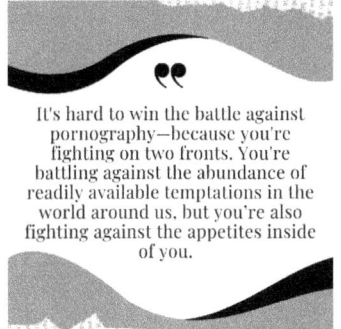
It's hard to win the battle against pornography—because you're fighting on two fronts. You're battling against the abundance of readily available temptations in the world around us, but you're also fighting against the appetites inside of you.

Even when we determine that we want to overcome this sin and eliminate it from our lives, the appetite doesn't immediately go away. That's one of the reasons it's so hard to win the battle against pornography—because you're fighting on two fronts. You're battling against the abundance of readily available temptations in the world around us, but you're also fighting against the appetites inside of you.

If you really want to obey Paul's teaching in Philippians 4:8, you must first control your appetites inside your heart and mind.

How do you do that?

In the last chapter, we discussed the need to analyze yourself and identify your weak and vulnerable areas. This helps you be aware of the times, situations, and circumstances when your appetites are most in control.

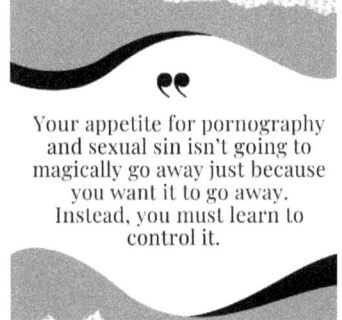

Your appetite for pornography and sexual sin isn't going to magically go away just because you want it to go away. Instead, you must learn to control it.

It's like someone who is on a diet. One of the first questions you'll need to ask is, *"When are you most likely to snack and eat junk food?"* After you've answered this question, then you use this knowledge to create a plan to overcome the temptation to cheat on your diet at your most vulnerable times.

The same principles apply to your appetite for pornography and sexual sin. It isn't going to magically go away just because you want it to. Instead, you must learn to control it. In this chapter, we will discuss some practical ways to do this.

Starting with:

You need to starve your appetite.

Here's the thing: pornography is not something you can play around with. You can't cut back a little and hope your appetite will decrease. It won't.

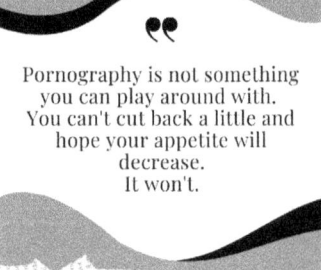

Pornography is not something you can play around with. You can't cut back a little and hope your appetite will decrease. It won't.

Because any exposure to pornography increases your appetite, you need to go cold turkey and completely starve this appetite by eliminating as many avenues of sexual content from your brain as humanly possible. Remember the definition of pornography. You need to eliminate this from your life if you want to be free.

Tools To Help You Overcome

One way to do this is to take a media fast.

For one month, do not watch any TV or any movies. Avoid all secular music and stay off of social media. Instead, take that time and spend it reading the Bible. At the end of the month, you will be surprised how little TV your conscience will allow you to watch after renewing your mind.

Is it extreme? Yes. But winning this battle is extremely serious.

Like a food cleanse is temporary as it removes all toxins from your body, a temporary media fast is an excellent way to remove toxins from your heart and mind as well as starve your appetite for pornography.

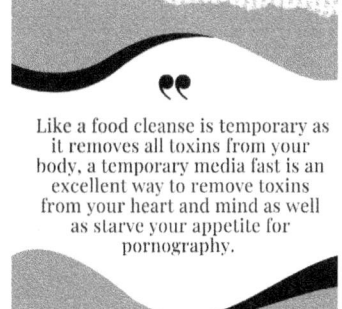

> Like a food cleanse is temporary as it removes all toxins from your body, a temporary media fast is an excellent way to remove toxins from your heart and mind as well as starve your appetite for pornography.

Plus, it's only thirty days—I promise you will survive.

But I get it; not everyone can or will be able to complete a full thirty-day media cleanse. It's a great idea that many people encourage, but when I was breaking free over twenty-five years ago, it wasn't an option. Instead, here's what I did during this time to starve my appetites:

- I only watched television with a *"G"* or *"PG"* rating for years.

- I stopped watching all romantic movies—even cheesy Hallmark ones—because they fed into my appetite for romance and a relationship that was not part of my life then. For me, it was like walking through an ice cream store, knowing I was lactose intolerant. Why torture myself? So, for a time—I eliminated this from my life.

- I stopped listening to all secular music.

- I stopped reading all fiction—even Christian fiction. Instead, I spent time in God's Word.

- I did not go to the movies.

- I stopped reading all secular magazines. (It's amazing how much pornography is in mainstream secular women's magazines.)

The point is that for years, I didn't allow any *"picture, film, or writing that caused sexual excitement"* into my life at all. I literally starved the appetite so that it would decrease and not control my life. I made sure the media I consumed was family-friendly, contained no sexual content, and adhered to the principles of Philippians 4:8. Even after I allowed myself to start watching *"chick flicks"* again, I mostly watched the Hallmark channel or very old black and white movies.

Now, as I said before, this was over twenty-five years ago, and we were living in a whole other world. If I remember correctly, we didn't even have the internet at our house, and social media didn't exist. I recognize that it is harder for women today as technology has created so many more opportunities for pornography to infect our lives. Yet, the principles remain the same—if you want to overcome, you must starve the appetite. This may mean:

- Deleting your social media accounts
- Telling your friends to stop sharing videos and memes
- Cancelling your streaming services
- Stop playing video games

The possibilities for tempting stimuli are endless. Only you know your weak areas and vulnerabilities, so you know what to eliminate. You must identify the areas that cause you the most temptation and do all you can to avoid them.

Tools To Help You Overcome

Take whatever steps are necessary to live sexually pure. Do what you need to do to obey Jesus' instructions in Matthew 5:27-30:

> *You have heard the commandment that says, 'You must not commit adultery.'*
>
> *But I say, anyone who even looks at a woman with lust has already committed adultery with her in his heart.*
>
> *So if your eye—even your good eye—causes you to lust, gouge it out and throw it away. It is better for you to lose one part of your body than for your whole body to be thrown into hell.*
>
> *And if your hand—even your stronger hand—causes you to sin, cut it off and throw it away. It is better for you to lose one part of your body than for your whole body to be thrown into hell. (NLT)*

First, we need to make the obvious point that Jesus wasn't suggesting self-mutilation—don't literally cut off your hand. Jesus was saying we are better off getting rid of whatever causes us to sin, even if it hurts, than allowing that sin to remain in our lives and separate us from God.

If pornography on the internet causes you to sin, get rid of any use of the internet in private. Only use it in a public setting where you'd be humiliated to be caught watching porn.

If TV or movies cause you to stumble, cancel your cable and Netflix. It is better to miss the latest reality show than to lose your soul.

Does secular music cause you to sin? Don't listen to it. It's better not to know the latest Taylor Swift or Beyonce song than to lose your soul eternally.

If you want to overcome sexual temptation, this is the standard you'll need to apply to starve your appetites so they don't control your life.

I can hear it now: *"C'mon, Adessa, let's get real." I agree that I can starve the areas that are causing me to sin, but I can't completely avoid television, movies, the internet, and social media for the rest of my life."*

This is true.

Obviously, just like you can't stay on a food cleanse forever, eventually, you have to eat; as you become stronger in your stand against pornography, you will be able to allow more forms of media back into your life. Over time, you'll need to set up boundaries and standards that say, *"This is what I will consume, and this is what I will not consume."*

One standard that we've agreed to in our house is that there will be absolutely no sex scenes in any show allowed in our home. Years ago, our pastor's wife, Devi Titus, taught that whenever you see a couple in bed together, you are watching pornography. Her teaching became a rule at our house. Whenever a program turns toward a bedroom scene or a couple starts undressing, we turn it off or fast forward. We do not need those images replaying in our minds.

Another commitment we've made is that if we accidentally encounter a program with a sexually explicit topic or unnecessarily crude language, we immediately turn it off. This is the power that will help you keep your mind pure: you have the right to stop watching or listening to entertainment that does not follow the guidelines of Philippians 4:8.

The good news is that there are tools available to help you keep these commitments.

Tools To Help You Overcome

The bad thing about technology is the enemy has figured out how to use it for destructive attacks against people's purity. The good thing about technology is that godly people have learned ways to safeguard against the enemies' attacks. Lots of tools are available to help.

Years ago, the first thing I would have suggested was using the V-chip on your television to block sexual content. However, while televisions still have V-chips, streaming service have made this *"one-size-fits-all"* asset irrelevant.

Instead, the best way to block inappropriate content is by using the Parental Controls offered by each streaming service. The good news is that almost all streaming services offer a Parental Control Option that you can set to PG and block out specific content. The challenge is that you need to investigate how to set the controls on each individual streaming service. This information can be found with a simple internet search.

Is this a hassle to set up? Yes.

However, it is worth the time and effort because it helps keep sexually explicit content out of your house. It's good protection for you and your family. Having to enter a password to watch a show is an excellent tool because it's like a big flashing *"Danger"* sign that makes you choose whether or not you want to risk the temptation. I highly recommend this on all televisions.

Another great tool is *VidAngel,* which removes sex and nudity from movies and TV shows. With *VidAngel* you can *"skip and mute the stuff you don't want to see or hear in your thousands of movies and TV shows, like profanity, nudity, violence and more."* They have the technology to remove content and make shows that we ordinarily need to avoid watchable.

Another tool is *TVGuardian Set-top Boxes for TV and Movies.* It automatically detects and filters profanity and other offensive phrases while you watch movies or television shows. *TVGuardian* is like a smart remote control for your TV that automatically mutes foul language. I have a friend who has used it for years, and she highly recommends it. They also have an option for streaming services called *TVG+*.

Another option is to choose streaming services like *PureFlix* or *Frndly*, which say they only promote family-friendly content.

Here's another important tip: **Use the parental controls available on all internet browsers.**

There are programs like *Net Nanny* or *Covenant Eyes* that you can install on your computer and devices. *Covenant Eyes* (**https://covenanteyes/mantour**) not only keeps you from being able to view porn on the internet, but they also send out email alerts to the accountability partner you choose to be accountable to, telling them what your web activity includes. When using these programs, remember to install them on your smartphones and tablets.

Another great option to help keep pornography out of your life is with a *CleanRouter*. *CleanRouter* blocks pornography from ever entering your home, church, or business. Instead of installing it on all your devices, it is installed on your network, so any device that uses your network, whether a smart TV, computer, phone, or tablet, is protected.

"But these things all cost money. I can't afford it."

I hear that every time I tell someone about these resources. Then they ask if I know of any free resources.

Let me say, first of all, there are no free Christian resources.

Secondly, **you can't afford NOT to use these programs if you're struggling with porn. It may take sacrificing other things to pay for it, but victory is worth the cost.**

Tools To Help You Overcome

The reason they cost money is simple: Someone had to develop the program, update it, and maintain it, and this costs money. They are not non-profits; they charge to cover their expenses. The worker is worthy of their hire.

The question you need to ask yourself is, *"If you went to the doctor and he told you that you were going to die unless you took a pill that cost $20-30 a month, could you find the money?"* What would you sacrifice to take that pill?

Straight talk: your spiritual, emotional, and mental health are at stake. Sexual sin can kill your relationship with God, your marriage, endanger your relationship with your kids, and every other relationship in your life. Like a life-saving pill, you can't afford NOT to use these programs to help you overcome. I would go as far as to say that if you can't afford the programs to keep you safe from sexual sin, then you can't afford cable, streaming services, or high-speed internet. It's that important.

I encourage you to take advantage of these technological advancements. It may cost you something, but freedom is worth the price.

> If you can't afford the programs to keep you safe from sexual sin, then you can't afford cable, streaming services, or high-speed internet. It's that important.

Of course, even the best technology will not leave you without choices. Ultimately, it will be up to you to decide whether you will starve the appetites for pornography or continue to feed them.

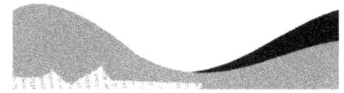

As we've said many times before, this won't be a one-time choice. Instead, you'll have to make these choices over and over again throughout your life to starve your appetite for pornography and sexual sin and, instead, wholeheartedly follow God's standards for sexuality.

Now, I'm not going to say this will be easy. I'd be lying if I said that a movie on *PureFlix* is as good as the latest movie from your Hollywood heartthrob. We all know it isn't.

Christian fiction can sometimes seem pretty cheesy compared to a steamy romance novel.

Often, we can feel like a person munching on rice cakes while the rest of the world is eating *Doritos* as we choose to replace the inappropriate sexual content that is common in our world with entertainment choices that conform to Biblical standards.

Sometimes, the struggle is real.

Let's be honest—this struggle is nothing compared to the challenges experienced by a woman who decides she is going to stop sleeping with her boyfriend and live an abstinent life until marriage, as the Bible says.

The woman who chooses to get her own place in response to the Holy Spirit's conviction about living with her boyfriend before marriage is going to experience loneliness. Not to mention that all the financial and other responsibilities now rest entirely on her. God bless her if she has to move back in with her parents.

The fact is that choosing to wholeheartedly follow Jesus and obey the Bible's teachings on sex and purity isn't easy. There will be times as you're starving your appetites and learning new ways to think that you'll think, *"This absolutely stinks."*

It reminds me of a few years ago when my Dad was first diagnosed with diabetes. After my Mom passed away, he stopped eating healthy food and binged on junk food, candy, and soda. Then, one day, his doctor gave him the bad news, and he had to change.

Tools To Help You Overcome

When he met with a dietician, they didn't just give him a list of foods he could eat and a list of what he could not. They also suggested *"replacement foods."*

Here's the thing—those replacement foods did not taste as good as what he was eating before.

However—they also weren't slowly killing him.

Eventually, he got used to the replacements. His appetites changed, and he was able to tolerate things like diet iced tea and artificial sweeteners. Now, he uses these things without really thinking about it.

This is the hope for everyone who is struggling as they starve their appetites and follow God's ways. Even though it isn't easy at first, over time, your appetites will adjust, and it will be easier.

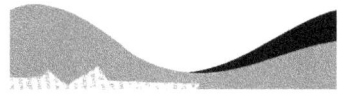

> This is the hope for everyone who is struggling as they starve their appetites and follow God's ways. Even though it isn't easy at first, over time, your appetites will adjust, and it will be easier.

Eventually, living by God's standards will become normal to you, and the struggle will not always be so difficult.

You need to remember throughout the process that, yes, making changes is hard, but you're doing it for a reason.

Pornography and sexual sin are your enemy. Like sugar to a person with diabetes, they are a poison that seeks to destroy your heart and mind.

> Pornography and sexual sin are your enemy. Like sugar to a person with diabetes, they are a poison that seeks to destroy your heart and mind.

Is fighting this battle easy? No.

Do you want to change your appetites? Probably not.

Do you want to pay money every month for things like *VidAngel* and *Covenant Eyes*? No one does.

However, you do these things so that you can have a healthy mind, heart, and soul.

You do them for your spiritual health, your mental health, and the health of your relationships.

Most importantly, you make these choices because you love God, you want to please Him, and follow His instructions to: **Fix your thoughts on what is true, and honorable, and right, and pure, and lovely, and admirable. Think about things that are excellent and worthy of praise. -Philippians 4:8, (NLT)**

# Group Study Questions...

1. What is the definition of *"pornography"*?

2. Why is *"soft pornography,"* as seen on television, in movies, in romance novels, or on social media, dangerous to our minds and souls? Why is it especially dangerous for women?

3. Define the word *"appetite"*.

4. How does knowing the definitions of *"pornography"* and *"appetite"* help us overcome sexual sin?

5. How is the battle against pornography fought on two fronts?

6. Read Matthew 5:27-30. How does Jesus' teaching in these verses relate to overcoming pornography and sexual sin?

7. What good fences can we establish for our media viewing that determine what will and will not be allowed in our homes?

8. Has anyone in the group used accountability software? What has worked for you? Why is *"I can't afford it"* not a valid excuse when it comes to using accountability software?

 ## Questions to Answer Privately....

1. How do you define *"pornography"*?

2. Do you believe that *"soft porn"* is pornography?

3. What did the analysis you did in the last chapter reveal to you about your appetites?

4. What do you need to do to starve the appetite for pornography and sexual sin in your life so that you can obey Jesus' teaching in Matthew 5:27-30?

5. This chapter shared two rules we have established as standards for the content we will not watch in our home. What regulations or boundaries will you set for yourself and your family regarding media content?

6. How do you feel about this statement: *"If you can't afford the programs to keep you safe from sexual sin, then you can't afford cable, streaming services, or high-speed internet. It's that important."*?

7. What can you rearrange in your budget to benefit from accountability software?

 *Take a moment and reread these key sentences, then journal what they mean to you.*

1. Pornography is any picture or writing that causes sexual excitement or that arouses a quick, intense emotional reaction.[1]

2. From the first moment that we see any pornography, it creates an appetite inside of us to see more. Every time we feed this appetite, our hunger for pornography increases.

3. It's hard to win the battle against pornography—because you're fighting on two fronts. You're battling against the abundance of readily available temptations in the world around us but also fighting against the appetites inside of you.

Tools To Help You Overcome

4. Your appetite for pornography and sexual sin isn't going to magically go away just because you want it to. Instead, you must learn to control it.

5. Pornography is not something you can play around with. You can't cut back a little and hope your appetite will decrease. It won't. Because any exposure to pornography increases your appetite, you need to go cold turkey and completely starve this appetite by eliminating as many avenues of sexual content from your brain as humanly possible.

6. If you can't afford the programs to keep you safe from sexual sin, then you can't afford cable, streaming services, or high-speed internet. It's that important.

 ## Scriptures to focus on and memorize...

How can a young man keep his way pure? By guarding it according to your word. -Psalm 119:9 (ESV)

No temptation has overtaken you that is not common to man. God is faithful, and he will not let you be tempted beyond your ability, but with the temptation he will also provide the way of escape, that you may be able to endure it. -1Corinthians 10:13 (ESV)

So put to death the sinful, earthly things lurking within you. Have nothing to do with sexual immorality, impurity, lust, and evil desires. Don't be greedy, for a greedy person is an idolater, worshiping the things of this world. -Colossians 3:5 (NLT)

Chapter Six
You Gotta Fight For Your Right To Purity

Ok, full disclosure…props to my brother, Jamie for this chapter title! I couldn't pass on it after he suggested it.

Anyway, as much as I believe that the tools mentioned in the last chapter help us fight the battle against sexual sin, it is equally important that we recognize that overcoming sexual temptation is a spiritual battle. As such, we need to rely heavily on the spiritual weapons God has given us to fight and win this battle in our minds.

As it says in Ephesians 6:12-13:

> *For we are not fighting against flesh-and-blood enemies, but against evil rulers and authorities of the unseen world, against mighty powers in this dark world, and against evil spirits in the heavenly places.*

> *Therefore, put on every piece of God's armor so you will be able to resist the enemy in the time of evil. Then after the battle you will still be standing firm. (NLT)*

In this chapter, we will discuss some of the essential spiritual weapons that God has given us to fight the battle against sexual sin.

1. Prayer.

Sometimes, we have to stop standing toe-to-toe and drop to our knees. When it comes to resisting temptation, prayer is a powerful tool.

As Jesus said, *"Watch and pray that you may not enter into temptation. The spirit indeed is willing, but the flesh is weak." -Matthew 26:41, (ESV)*

Paul lists prayer among the spiritual weapons as he talks about the whole armor of God.

> *Therefore take up the whole armor of God, that you may be able to withstand in the evil day, and having done all, to stand firm.*
>
> *Stand therefore, having fastened on the belt of truth, and having put on the breastplate of righteousness, and, as shoes for your feet, having put on the readiness given by the gospel of peace. In all circumstances take up the shield of faith, with which you can extinguish all the flaming darts of the evil one; and take the helmet of salvation, and the sword of the Spirit, which is the word of God, praying at all times in the Spirit, with all prayer and supplication. -Ephesians 6:13-18, (ESV)*

Praying to resist temptation is even included in the Lord's prayer.

> *And lead us not into temptation, but deliver us from evil. -Matthew 6:13, (ESV)*

When we pray, we acknowledge our dependence on God. When we pray according to God's will (and trust me, resisting temptation is God's will), we have the promise that God will hear and help us.

> *And this is the confidence that we have toward him, that if we ask anything according to his will he hears us. And if we know that he hears us in whatever we ask, we know that we have the requests that we have asked of him. -1 John 5:14-15, (ESV)*

Other prayers that we know are God's will are:

- Asking God for strength to fight the battle against temptation.

- Ask God to deliver you from your sexual sin and to set you free from the grip of bondage it has on you.

- Praying for wisdom and discernment so you will make wise choices as you walk in freedom.

> *If any of you lacks wisdom, let him ask God, who gives generously to all without reproach, and it will be given him. -James 1:5, (ESV)*

Of course, confessing our sins as we pray is a powerful weapon in the battle against sexual sin. But we don't have to wait until we've fallen into sin to ask God to forgive us. We can go to God when we feel tempted, when the first thought of entering into sin pops into our minds. Even if we accidentally see something that stirs up an appetite inside of us, we can go to God, confess what happened, and ask Him to forgive us and give us the strength to overcome.

If we sin, we must ask God to forgive us immediately. It's important to keep a short balance sheet with God. Any time even a thought or desire to sin sexually or watch pornography pops up, cast it down in Jesus' name. Confess it and move on, continuing the pursuit of sexual purity.

If you don't know what to pray, try speaking in tongues.

> ***Likewise the Spirit helps us in our weakness. For we do not know what to pray for as we ought, but the Spirit himself intercedes for us with groanings too deep for words. -Romans 8:26 (ESV)***

This brings us to the next point:

2. **Rely on the Holy Spirit**

Jesus promised to send us a helper. That helper is the Holy Spirit.

The Holy Spirit cannot be joined with unholy spirits. His holiness cannot take the unholiness. Ask the Holy Spirit to lead and guide your life, and stay sensitive to His convicting power.

> ***But I say, walk by the Spirit, and you will not gratify the desires of the flesh. For the desires of the flesh are against the Spirit, and the desires of the Spirit are against the flesh, for these are opposed to each other, to keep you from doing the things you want to do. -Galatians 5:16-17 (ESV)***

Ask the Holy Spirit for help developing self-control and resisting temptation. Stay sensitive to His conviction; don't ignore it. We grow spiritually by allowing the Holy Spirit's power to work within us.

As we said in our first point, speaking in tongues is another way to rely on the Holy Spirit to help us overcome temptation. You see, as a Christian, the Holy Spirit lives inside you. When you use the gift of the baptism in the Holy Spirit and pray in tongues, you are literally "stirring up" the Holy Spirit's power inside of you, empowering you to fight and overcome sin in your life.

As Romans 8:11-12 says:

> *The Spirit of God, who raised Jesus from the dead, lives in you. And just as God raised Christ Jesus from the dead, he will give life to your mortal bodies by this same Spirit living within you.*
>
> *Therefore, dear brothers and sisters, you have no obligation to do what your sinful nature urges you to do. (NLT)*

That's how using your prayer language and speaking in tongues helps you overcome temptation.

3. Devour the Word of God

The best way to remove the sexual thoughts and perversion that pornography and sexual sin cause in your mind is to soak your mind in God's Word. Renew your mind with God's Word.

> *Do not be conformed to this world, but be transformed by the renewal of your mind, that by testing you may discern what is the will of God, what is good and acceptable and perfect. -Romans 12:2 (ESV)*

Meditate on Scriptures that help you develop a pure mindset. It is hard to sin sexually while reading the Word of God. It is hard to think of impure thoughts if you are thinking the thoughts of God found in His Word. When you spend time in the Word, you will gain victory.

If you're serious about overcoming temptation, you can go beyond reading God's Word and commit to memorizing Scripture.

How does this help?

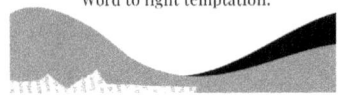

> When you memorize Scripture, you make a spiritual deposit in your mental savings account. When you feel tempted to fall into sin, the Holy Spirit can bring the Scripture you deposited to the forefront of your mind so that you can follow Jesus' example and use God's Word to fight temptation.

When you memorize Scripture, you make a spiritual deposit in your mental savings account. When you feel tempted to fall into sin, the Holy Spirit can bring the Scripture you deposited to the forefront of your mind so that you can follow Jesus' example and use God's Word to fight temptation. (Matthew 4:1-11)

But here's the thing—the Holy Spirit can't remind you of Scriptures you haven't read or memorized. So make sure your arsenal is full in your battle against temptation—while fighting for your freedom, spend as much time as possible in God's Word.

4. Worship

Hmmm…you don't hear that much when people talk about overcoming sexual temptation. Yet, it is a valuable tool.

Let me begin by saying that I encourage anyone who is fighting the battle against sexual temptation and sexual sin to stop listening to all secular music. Do your best to cut it out of your life.

Why?

Most secular music focuses on romance and sexuality from a worldly perspective. Many secular songs are downright disgusting in their portrayal of sex and women. That's why I believe it's one of the things you should eliminate from your life while you are in the heat of this battle.

Instead, fill the void with praise and worship music. This will help you in several ways:

First, worship music leads you into the completely holy presence of God. The more comfortable you are spending time in God's presence, the less comfortable you will be with perversion or sin.

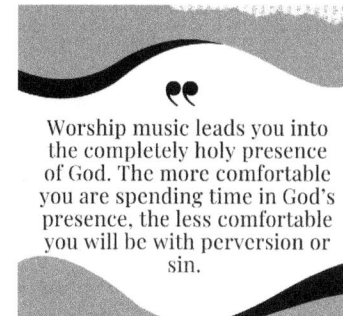

> Worship music leads you into the completely holy presence of God. The more comfortable you are spending time in God's presence, the less comfortable you will be with perversion or sin.

Worship is the music of spiritual warfare. Praise is a weapon we can use to fight spiritual battles. Like reading God's Word, it's really difficult to sin sexually while you are praising God. So add worship to your battle arsenal in your fight against the enemy.

5. Read & Learn

You are not alone in your fight against temptation, sin, and battling strongholds in your mind. Thankfully, those who have already won this battle have shared the secrets to their success. Here are some resources that will help you:

-*Covenant Eyes* has many books and blogs available for women. You can check them out at: **covenanteyes.com**.

-*Covenant Eyes* also has a 21-day Email Detox for women called *"Arise."*

"Arise is a 21-day journey toward sexual healing within a safe, confidential community of women. Walk through daily videos with our host, Beth Davis, as she uses her story and those of other women to speak hope into yours. Here's what you can expect:

-*Biblical truth blended with modern counseling methods to help you heal*

-*A self-guided pace so you can go through one session a day or linger as God leads*

-Daily activities, worksheets, and reflections to help you apply what you learn." [1]

-Pure Life Ministries offers many books and blogs that can help you overcome pornography and sexual sin, including one, especially for women, *"Create in Me a Pure Heart"* by Kathy Gallagher. I have not read this book, but Lisa Bevere recommends it.

-I also recommend *"Victory's Journey"* by Laverne Weber to help you address the root causes of your issues.

-Another book I've written is *"Mind-Blowing Truths: Demolishing The Strongholds In Your Life"*, which will help you overcome hidden sin and get to the root cause of the sin in your life.

6. Choose to take your thoughts captive.

2 Corinthians 10:5 tells us that we need to take our thoughts captive.

> **We destroy arguments and every lofty opinion raised against the knowledge of God, and take every thought captive to obey Christ. (ESV)**

This means that you literally recognize ungodly thoughts as they enter your mind and choose not to entertain them but to think another way.

Here's an example:

Recently, I was texting with a friend who was taking some classes. She had previously shared with me that she knew these classes were the next step in fulfilling God's plan for her life. When I asked her how her classes were going, I was surprised to hear that she'd stopped taking them. When I asked, "Why?" She said she was afraid. Whenever she took a class, someone in her family had a health issue.

I immediately felt the Holy Spirit lead me to say, *"That's superstition. These thoughts are lies from the enemy trying to keep you from doing what you know you should do."* We continued talking. I shared some Scriptures and told her to call me the next time she was afraid, and we'd pray together.

Sounds pretty spiritual, right?? Good job, Adessa!

But here's the funny thing: a few days later, I was walking down the same path of fear. As I prepared to do something, I could only think, *"The last time we did this, something bad happened—maybe we shouldn't do it again."*

Immediately, I remembered my words to my friend: that's superstition—God doesn't want His children living in fear.

Now it was my turn to choose to *"take my thought captive"* and say, *"Hey, you crazy thought. Get out of my head. You are a liar. You can't stay here."*

Then, I followed Jesus' example when He was tempted and used God's Word to show these thoughts the way out the door.

> ***For God has not given us a spirit of fear; but of power and of love and of a sound mind. -2 Timothy 1:7 (NKJV)***

> ***The Lord directs the steps of the godly. He delights in every detail of their lives. -Psalm 37:23 (NLT)***

That's what it means to *"take your thoughts captive."* It's the pattern we need to follow when ungodly thoughts of lust fill our minds or when our appetites are screaming, *"Feed me now!!!"*

We need to take control of our minds and say, *"No, I'm not going to think this way. I'm not entertaining this thought. I won't dwell here and let my mind fantasize or think impure thoughts. And we are absolutely not falling into sin just because my mind suggested it. Instead,*

WHATEVER IS LOVELY

I'm serving this thought notice—you're not welcome here. Get out of my mind NOW!"

Then, you force yourself to start thinking of something else. Sing a praise song. Read the Bible. Call a friend or your accountability partner on the phone. Do something that gets your mind off the tempting thoughts and resist temptation.

This brings us to our next point:

7. When all else fails, RUN!

> ***I Corinthians 6:18 says, "Flee from sexual immortality. Every other sin a person commits is outside the body, but the sexually immoral person sins against his own body." (ESV)***

In this verse, the Bible literally tells us to flee from anything that focuses on the sensual, sexual, or arouses ungodly desires inside of us.

The Bible literally tells us to flee from anything that focuses on the sensual, sexual, or arouses ungodly desires inside of us.

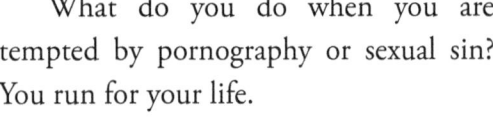

What do you do when you are tempted by pornography or sexual sin? You run for your life.

Follow Joseph's example of running from Potiphar's wife in Genesis 39 and get out of there!

If we try to reason with lust or entertain sexual thoughts, we will give in to them. We won't be able to fight it. This is why God forcefully orders us to run away from it.

Run with all your might.

Again, this can be so practical.

If you are tempted to fall into temptation with pornography, get up and do something else.

Find some people to be around.

Contact a friend.

Get up and go for some ice cream.

Start a project.

Call your accountability partner and ask that they pray with you.

Run away from the temptation like your life depended on it, ask the Holy Spirit for strength, and resist.

Pray.

Speak in tongues.

Read the Bible.

Quote Scripture like Jesus did.

Do everything you can to resist the enemy, and he will flee.

> *Submit yourselves therefore to God. Resist the devil, and he will flee from you. (James 4:7, ESV)*

Use the spiritual weapons that God has given you, and FIGHT!

Overcoming sexual sin is a lifelong battle for many, but with God's help, persistent prayer, and practical steps, victory is possible. However, I must be honest—you will only win the battle and gain victory over sexual temptation if you choose to FIGHT!

You will only win the battle and gain victory over sexual temptation if you choose to FIGHT!

Someone once asked my brother, *"If overcoming sexual sin is as easy as the steps listed above, then why are so many people living in defeat?"*

The answer is simple: The steps only work if they are followed and they are challenging.

Confessing your sin to an accountability partner and being vulnerable with them is hard.

Watching and listening to whatever you want is easier than limiting your media consumption.

Accountability software costs money.

Going to a counselor costs time and money.

Investing time in prayer and God's Word takes time and sacrifice.

Quite honestly, sexual sin offers momentary pleasure.

Sadly, the reason that so many of God's people are trapped in the bondage of sexual sin is that they choose not to fight for freedom.

This is an option. Many have chosen to walk away from the fight, and live bond by sexual sin their whole lives.

But personally, I am tired of watching people make that choice. I'm so tired of being heartbroken, watching people's lives torn apart by the destruction of pornography and sexual sin.

That's why I wrote this book—which, honestly, I never wanted to write…to encourage you to fight for your freedom.

To help you choose to use the tools God has given us to overcome.

The fact is that I don't want to see any woman wake up five, ten, or twenty years down the road and think, *"What would have happened if I'd been strong enough to fight?"*

Freedom is available to you today.

There is hope.

You Gotta Fight For Your Right To Purity

As we said in the beginning, God wants you to be free. He's given you all that you need.

Now the choice is up to you.

Will you stand and fight?

Will you stop making excuses, stop choosing to coddle your sin, and say, *"Whatever it takes, I am going to fight for my freedom?"*

You can do it.

I won this battle in my life over twenty-five years ago, so I know it is possible.

The choice rests with you—are you willing to do whatever it takes to fight for your freedom?

 *Group Study Questions...*

1. Read Ephesians 6:12-13. How is the fight to overcome sexual temptation a spiritual battle?

2. How does prayer help us fight temptation and overcome an addiction to pornography and sexual sin?

3. How can using our prayer language and praying in tongues help us gain victory?

4. What role does the Holy Spirit play in helping us overcome temptation and sin?

5. How can memorizing Scripture help you during times of temptation?

6. Explain worship music's role in spiritual warfare and winning the battle against sin.

7. Why is it a good idea to give up listening to secular music as you are fighting the battle to overcome sexual sin?

8. What does it mean to *"take your thoughts captive"*?

Questions to Answer Privately....

1. Have you ever thought of your battle to overcome pornography and sexual sin as a spiritual battle?

2. As you read this chapter, did the Holy Spirit point out any specific spiritual disciplines you need to focus on?

3. Do you regularly spend time in prayer? If not, let's plan to make that a part of your life. Start by taking an honest look at your life and schedule and asking:

   -When is a good time for me to pray?

   -Where's a quiet, private place for me to pray?

   -Is this place comfortable? Is it somewhere I will want to go?

   -Is it distraction-free? If not, how can I remove distractions?

   Once you've made a plan, put it on your schedule and keep your appointment each day.

4. Are you baptized in the Holy Spirit or actively pursuing the baptism in the Holy Spirit? If so, have you tried praying in tongues to fight temptation?

5. Are you spending time each day in God's Word? If not, how can you create a plan to start?

6. Will you commit to memorizing at least one Scripture a week? The verses at the end of each chapter provide a good place to start.

7. Are you willing to eliminate secular music from your life and replace it with worship music?

8. Looking back at the vulnerable areas we discussed in previous chapters, list five practical ways to *"flee temptation"* the next time it arises. Be specific—where you can go and who you can call.

    1.

    2.

    3.

    4.

    5.

Take a moment and reread these key sentences, then journal what they mean to you.

1. Overcoming sexual temptation is a spiritual battle. As such, we need to rely heavily on the spiritual weapons God has given us to fight and win this battle in our minds.

2. When you memorize Scripture, you make a spiritual deposit in your mental savings account. When you feel tempted to fall into sin, the Holy Spirit can bring the Scripture you deposited to the forefront of your mind so that you can follow Jesus' example and use God's Word to fight temptation. (Matthew 4:1-11)

3. Worship is the music of spiritual warfare. Praise is a weapon we can use to fight spiritual battles.

4. If we try to reason with lust or entertain sexual thoughts, we will give in to them. We won't be able to fight it. This is why God forcefully orders us to run away from it.

 Scriptures to focus on and memorize...

For we are not fighting against flesh-and-blood enemies, but against evil rulers and authorities of the unseen world, against mighty powers in this dark world, and against evil spirits in the heavenly places.

Therefore, put on every piece of God's armor so you will be able to resist the enemy in the time of evil. Then after the battle you will still be standing firm. -Ephesians 6:12-13 (NLT)

Watch and pray that you may not enter into temptation. The spirit indeed is willing, but the flesh is weak. -Matthew 26:41 (ESV)

And this is the confidence that we have toward him, that if we ask anything according to his will he hears us. And if we know that he hears us in whatever we ask, we know that we have the requests that we have asked of him. -1 John 5:14-15 (ESV)

We destroy arguments and every lofty opinion raised against the knowledge of God, and take every thought captive to obey Christ. -2 Corinthians 10:5 (ESV)

Submit yourselves therefore to God. Resist the devil, and he will flee from you. -James 4:7 (ESV)

Chapter Seven
Final Thoughts

Recently, a friend reminded me that one of the biggest struggles that keeps people trapped in sexual sin is hopelessness and feeling like they can never gain victory. Before we wrap up our study, I feel like I'd be remiss if I didn't leave you with one final note of challenging encouragement and hope. It is from Ephesians 6:10:

> *A final word: Be strong in the Lord and in his mighty power. (NLT)*

Throughout this study, we've talked about many spiritual disciplines and tools that will help you win the battle against pornography and sexual temptation. Let me be clear: with the help of the Holy Spirit and your determination and commitment, you can gain complete and total victory and walk in freedom.

Yet, it's important to acknowledge that even after you've won your battle, even after you are free from the bondage and addiction that pornography holds its victims, even if you've been living in victory for years, you are still going to be living in this world that is filled with sexual images and messaging. There will be times when something will come across your path, knock at your door, and seek to draw you back into sin.

It happens to everyone. What do you do?

You stand firm. You use your spiritual disciplines.

You pray.

Quote the Scripture you've memorized.

Pray in tongues.

Turn on some worship music and flee temptation.

You say, *"Nope. No way, no how, not gonna happen, I'm not going back."*

Then, you stand your ground and resist temptation.

Here's a practical story from my own life that illustrates this principle.

It had been at least two decades since I'd done the work necessary to gain freedom. One summer, I was watching a very family-friendly show on the Hallmark Channel. As I watched, I thought, *"Wouldn't it be fun to read the book and the story on which it was based?"* So, I bought the Kindle version and prepared to enjoy it.

Only the books were quite different from the television show. Even though the characters were still intriguing and their dialogue was still rich, I was surprised to find profanity in the second or third chapter.

At first, it jarred me because there was no swearing on the show. But I tried to push it aside and told myself, *"Grow up, girl. It's not like you've never heard that phrase before; it's pretty mild. Just ignore it and move on."*

Final Thoughts

So I tried.

Only it wasn't long before I began sensing a larger problem looming in the storyline. You see, while the series I had been watching focused on love and family relationships, but the descriptions in the books emphasized attraction and sensuality. The author described the physical traits of love interests and the desires they aroused inside the characters. It was very sensual and erotic.

That's when I decided that it didn't matter if I wasted the money on the book or even if the storyline was really interesting. If I wanted to keep my heart and mind pure before God, I needed to stop reading it. I deleted it from all of my devices.

Why? Simply put, because I've been there and done that, I've seen the effect that this type of reading material (or books and movies) can have on my attitudes, feelings about myself, others, and even my relationship with God. I know the desire it stirs up inside, the images that are so hard to get out of your mind. I've seen the danger, and there is NO WAY I'm going to dip my toe in the water of that river again.

Each of us needs to do this to maintain our freedom and victory. When we encounter something or someone who wants to drag us back into the old traps we fought so hard to escape, we must be on our guard, resist temptation, and stand firm in the faith.

You might even want to ask God to forgive you for what you saw, read, or heard just to keep your conscience clean before Him. It wouldn't hurt to share what happened with a trusted friend or family member so that you don't give ground to hiding sin again.

Do whatever you need to do to stay free from temptation. Remember how hard you fought to be free and fight just as hard to remain free.

> *"Therefore, put on every piece of God's armor so you will be able to resist the enemy in the time of evil. Then after the battle you will still be standing firm."—Ephesians 6:13 (NLT)*

What do you do if you don't stand firm but fall back into temptation?

What if you don't stick to your plan, if you fall off the wagon, and go backward?

Ask God to forgive you and start again.

Confess your sin to God.

Confess to a trusted accountability partner.

Don't quit. Get back up, start again, and keep moving toward living as the woman of God that you are called to be.

Don't allow one misstep to take back all the ground you fought so hard to win. Instead, get back, brush yourself off, and continue to fight. Don't give up.

> *..for the righteous falls seven times and rises again..*
> *-Proverbs 24:16 (ESV)*

Get back up! Keep pursuing holiness even if you fall. God's grace is sufficient, and He will help you stand back up and get back into the fight.

The fact is that as long as we live in this world, we will always be fighting to keep our minds pure. However, it's important to remember that we can win this battle.

You only lose when you lie down and quit fighting.

Don't do that!

Final Thoughts

As 2 Thessalonians 3:13 says, ***"Do not grow weary in doing good." (ESV)***

As Paul challenged Timothy, today, I end this book by challenging you:

> *But you, Timothy, are a man of God; so run from all these evil things.*
>
> *Pursue righteousness and a godly life, along with faith, love, perseverance, and gentleness.*
>
> *Fight the good fight for the true faith.*
>
> *Hold tightly to the eternal life to which God has called you, which you have declared so well before many witnesses. -1 Timothy 6:11-12 (NLT)*

My dear sister, as Paul said to Timothy, you must remember that you are a woman of God.

> **Therefore, if anyone is in Christ, he is a new creation. The old has passed away; behold, the new has come. -2 Corinthians 5:17 (ESV)**

In Christ, you are forgiven, redeemed, and set free. Don't let shame or guilt destroy you. Instead, stand firm in the new identity God has given you.

Remember, as a child of God, you have all the power you need to defeat sexual sin.

> *I can do all things through him who strengthens me. -Philippians 4:13 (ESV)*

Standing firm in your identity as a child of God, you know that you have all the power inside of you that you need to:

- Run from all evil things

WHATEVER IS LOVELY

- Pursue righteousness
- Live a godly life, along with faith, love, perseverance, and gentleness
- Fight the good fight for the true faith
- Hold tightly to the eternal life to which God has called you

Just as Paul believed in Timothy, I believe in you.

I'm praying that God will give you all the strength, courage, and fortitude necessary to fight and win the battle against all forms of pornography and sexual sin and join the army of women who share their testimony of freedom.

You can do this!

Adessa Holden

Bibliography

Chapter 1

1. *CovenantEyes,* learn.covenanteyes.com/women/. Accessed 4 Oct. 2024.

2. "T H E P O R N P H E N O M E N O N: *The Impact of Pornography in the Digital Age."* Barna.Com, www.barna.com/the-porn-phenomenon/. Accessed 4 Oct. 2024.

3. Cowell, Maria. *"Porn: Women Use It Too."* Christianity Today, 8 Feb. 2015, www.christianitytoday.com/2015/02/porn-women-use-it-too/. Accessed 4 Oct. 2024.

4. "Porn Addiction Help for Women Online Resources, Support, and Community for Women Struggling with Porn and Sexual Integrity." XXXChurch, xxxchurch.com/get-help/porn-addiction-help-for-women. Accessed 4 Oct. 2024.

5. Lykins, Liz. *"Study Finds that More Than Half of Christians Use Porn—and They're Comfortable With It"* The Roys Report, 24, October, 2024, https://julieroys.com/study-finds-more-than-half-christians-use-porn-theyre-comfortable-it/. Accessed 14 November,. 2024.

Chapter 2

1. *"NIV Reverse Interlinear Bible: English to Hebrew and English to Greek. Copyright © 2019 by Zondervan."* BibleGateway, www.biblegateway.com/passage/search=Ephesians%204%3A3-5%20&version=NIV. Accessed 4 Oct. 2024.

2. Horton, Stanley M. *Systematic Theology: A Pentecostal Perspective.* Springfield, Mo: Logion Press, 1994. Print. Pg 128.

3. Childers, Alisa. *Live Your Truth and Other Lies.* E-book Edition. Tyndale Momentum, 2022.

Chapter 4

1. Donald C Stamps, *Study Notes on Hebrews 12, Fire Bible:* English Standard Version, (Peabody, MA: Hendrickson Publishers Marketing, LLC, 2014, Pg 2160.

2. *"A Sneeze, Detention, and Sissy Spacek."* Young Sheldon. Created by Chuck Lorre and Steven Molaro, Season 1 Episode 13, Chuck Lorre Productions, 2018.

Chapter 5

1. "Pornography, N. (1 & 3)." *Merriam-Webster,* https://www.merriam-webster.com/dictionary/pornography. Accessed 5 October 2024.

2. "Appetite", N. (C2)." *Cambridge Dictionary,* https://dictionary.cambridge.org/dictionary/english/appetite. Accessed 5 October 2024.

Chapter 6

1. "Email Challenges." Covenant Eyes, www.covenanteyes.com/e-mail-challenges/. Accessed 9 Oct. 2024.

Resources To Help You Fight!

TV/Streaming:

- VidAngel www.vidangel.com/

- TVGuardian Set-top Boxes for TV and Movies www.tvguardian.com/

- PureFlix www.pureflix.com/

- Frndly try.frndlytv.com/

Internet Tools:

- Covenant Eyes covenanteyes.com

- Net Nanny www.netnanny.com/

- CleanRouter cleanrouter.com/

Recommended Books:

- *Create in Me a Pure Heart* by Kathy Gallagher

- *Battlefield of the Mind* by Joyce Meyers

- *Victory's Journey* by Laverne Weber

- *Finding Healing* by Adessa Holden

- *Mind-Blowing: Truths: Steps to Healing* by Adessa Holden

- *Mind-Blowing Truths: Demolishing The Strongholds In Your Mind* by Adessa Holden

- *Broken Windows of the Soul: A Pastor and Christian Psychologist Discuss Sexual Sins and the Prescription to Heal Them* by Arnold R. Fleagle DMin and Donald A. Lichi Phd

Ebooks:

- Covenant Eyes offers a free e-book, *New Fruit: A Woman's Guide to Porn Recovery.* Download at: www.covenanteyes.com/solutions/quit-porn/women/.

Blogs:

- Covenant Eyes www.covenanteyes.com/blog/
- Pure Life Ministries www.purelifeministries.org/blog

Podcasts

- The Covenant Eyes Podcast www.podcasts.apple.com/us/podcast/the-covenant-eyes-podcast/id1608922111
- PureLife Ministries Podcast www.podcasts.apple.com/us/podcast/pure-life-ministries-podcast/id267006757

Resources:

- Covenant Eyes also has a 21-day Email Detox for women called. *Arise.* www.covenanteyes.com/arise/
- Covenant Eyes offers a FREE IN-APP COURSE, *The Unique Ways Women Struggle With Porn.* This course helps women understand why they turn to porn and some key ways to find

lasting freedom. www.covenanteyes.com/solutions/quit-porn/women/.

Christian Counselors:

• Beyond Survival Ministries—A Time to Heal Beyond Survival atimetohealbeyondsurvival.org.

• Pure Life Ministries' *Create in Me a Pure Heart Program* is a six-week program that includes audio or video counseling from home, with flexible counseling hours based on your schedule. Pricing and details are available at purelifeministries.org/struggling-women.

• Emerge Counseling Ministries offers a Biblically-based counseling perspective to help you overcome sexual sin and pornography is at emerge.org.

• Celebrate Recovery https://celebraterecovery.com/

IF YOU WOULD LIKE TO HAVE ADESSA SPEAK TO YOUR SMALL GROUP ON THIS TOPIC VIA ZOOM, CONTACT HER AT

www.adessaholden.com/adessa-speaker

ABOUT THE AUTHOR:

Adessa Holden is an ordained minister with the Assemblies of God, an author, a speaker, and a Bible teacher. She is a passionate individual who dedicates her life to these roles, inspiring others with her commitment.

Adessa is also the Vice President/Treasurer of 4One Ministries. She and her brother travel to speak, hold Mantour conferences, and produce resources. Their work provides practical Biblical teaching that strengthens, encourages, and challenges individuals to grow in their walk with Christ and apply Biblical principles to their everyday lives.

She graduated from the University of Valley Forge in 1996 with a degree in pastoral ministry and has continued studying God's Word ever since.

She's written *"Finding Healing," "The Adventure: Discovering Your God-Given Passion, Place, and Purpose,"* and *"Ageless Truths: Lessons I Learned in My Forties that I Wish I Knew In My Twenties."* She also co-wrote *"Whatever It Takes"* with her brother, Jamie.

She's excited to share her newest project, *"Mindblowing Truths,"* a series of topical Bible studies designed to help individuals and small groups learn the mind-blowing truths in God's Word and practically apply them in their lives.

If you ask her about herself, she will tell you, *"I'm a minister, an author, a sister, and a daughter. The most important thing in my life is my relationship with Jesus, which began when I was just five years old, and I hid behind the sofa in our house and asked Jesus into my heart. Two years later, I received my call into full-time ministry. Following Jesus and studying God's Word have been my passion throughout my life. It's my most incredible honor and privilege to share the testimony of the healing the Holy Spirit has done in my heart, the difficulties He's helped me overcome, and the truth I've learned from God's Word. My life's goal is to encourage others to develop a personal relationship with Jesus and experience God's freedom and healing for themselves. Using every means possible, I want to reach people for Jesus."*

Are you tired of facing the same struggles repeatedly? Do you feel trapped by anger, addiction, anxiety, or other challenges that control your life?

You are not alone. But here's the good news: there is hope. You can gain victory and become the person God wants you to be, fulfilling His purpose for your life.

Mind-Blowing Truths: Demolishing the Strongholds in Your Mind shares Biblical principles to overcome hidden thought patterns that keep you in bondage. This practical guide helps you identify root issues and partner with the Holy Spirit to gain freedom, victory, and hope.

Are you ready for the Holy Spirit to use the Word of God to blow your mind and set you free? This book is for you!

Visit adessaholden.com for details.

Available in print and digital formats.

In *Mind-blowing Truth: Steps to Healing*, you will discover steps and tools to partner with the Holy Spirit and find healing and victory in your life.

This practical study explains the steps to healing, how you can put them into practice, and even how you might feel or the struggles you may face along the way. Each chapter also has a workbook section with questions to answer, Scriptures to ponder and memorize, and a place to journal about what the Holy Spirit speaks to you.

This book offers you what you need most: hope and practical steps to healing.

Visit adessaholden.com for details.

Available in print and digital formats.

www.ingramcontent.com/pod-product-compliance
Lightning Source LLC
Chambersburg PA
CBHW050912160426
43194CB00011B/2372